NOVEMBER 2012

To THE BEST
BROTHER IN THE
WORLD.
LOVE YOU.
Barb ☺
(your oldest sister!

Trucking in British Columbia

Trucking in British Columbia
An Illustrated History

Daniel Francis

Harbour Publishing

CONTENTS

This truck could use a haircut. Farmhands haul a load of hay in the Fraser Valley, July 1944.
With essential supplies of rubber tires and gasoline being rationed, wartime was difficult for
truckers, who were doing important work to support the home front.

City of Vancouver Archives, CVA 586-2965, Don Coltman/Steffens Colmer photo

Foreword

This book chronicles the history of one of the most significant industries that shaped BC's past and will continue to influence BC's future. Over the past one hundred years, the trucking industry has grown from a handful of horseless carriages to a two-billion-dollar enterprise with over twenty thousand companies operating over fifty thousand trucks.

Much has changed in the last century in terms of highways, technology, equipment, fuel, government regulation, and communications, but the common theme that runs through the decades is that of the perseverance, ingenuity and dedication of the tens of thousands of men—and women—who committed themselves to serving their customers in communities throughout BC and beyond. Freight that doesn't arrive on time and in good shape is often worthless, so reliability has been critical to the growth and success of the industry. This is even truer in more recent times when "just-in-time" inventory systems have become commonplace.

Trucking is the essential link for all other modes of transportation—rail, air and sea—and transportation continues to be an essential success factor for a province whose economy is and ever has been export oriented. So until *Star Trek* teleporters become a reality, trucks—and the people who drive, dispatch, maintain and support them—will continue to play their key role in British Columbia life.

When thinking of meaningful ways to commemorate its hundredth anniversary, the BC Trucking Association, which first came into being as the General Cartage and Storage Association in 1913, decided it could do nothing better than sponsor a new history of the industry. The last was Andy Craig's pioneering 1977 book, *Trucking,* which deserved a follow-up since the industry has evolved immensely in the three decades since. While BCTA lent financial support for the project as our gift to the industry and BC, this book would never have gone past the drawing board stage without the independent participation, expertise and enthusiasm of award-winning author Daniel Francis and BC's own Harbour Publishing.

Through vignettes, stories and photos, *Trucking in British Columbia* unveils some of the quirky, stubborn, dedicated, independent, often daredevil, sometimes heroic, and always service-oriented men and women who make up an industry that touches each British Columbian every day. Even though the most visible and obvious aspect of the industry is trucks of all shapes and sizes, more than anything, trucking is about people. And it's the stories of those people that best illustrate the nature of the trucking industry, as Dan Francis ably demonstrates in the pages that follow, assisted by hundreds of photos from sources across the province.

I am confident this book will serve to commemorate trucking's amazing century of change in a way that can be enjoyed by all British Columbians, who are part of the trucking story whether they realize it or not.

Louise Yako
President and CEO
BC Trucking Association

A horse-drawn buggy, two trucks and a streetcar vie for space as evolving transportation technologies share the road on Main Street, Vancouver, in 1940. Vancouver Public Library 43410, Province photo

A Century of Trucking

One hundred years ago, when motor vehicles were replacing the horse-drawn wagon as the principal means of carrying freight, truck drivers were at the forefront of a transportation revolution. Like the explorers and fur traders of an earlier era, truckers were the pathfinders who opened up new routes through the interior of the province, connecting communities to each other and forging links between the metropolitan centres on the coast and the smaller towns and villages of the hinterland. The "Romance of the Road" was not just an advertising slogan; it meant something to the drivers who battled the elements with their loads and to the folks who relied on them to make it through.

Early freight trucks, with their hard rubber tires and wooden wheels, took over from horse-drawn wagons at about the time of World War I.
Royal BC Museum, BC Archives, D-09303

Early truckers had to cope with roads that were often no better than rutted tracks. Surprising as it may be to us today, before the 1920s it was not possible to drive from the coast of British Columbia to the Interior. The sole road that had once done the job, the famed Cariboo Road, was destroyed by railway construction and not rebuilt. Any venturesome trucker wishing to drive his Ford Model A one-ton with a load of freight to the Okanagan, the Kootenays or the Cariboo had to make a detour south through the United States first. It was 1927 before the Fraser Canyon Highway officially opened and long-haul trucking really got underway in the province.

Those early drivers had nerves of steel. The roads they followed were nothing but winding ribbons of dirt and gravel carved out of the mountainsides. At the best of times it was like taming a wild horse to drive one of the early trucks with their flimsy steering, solid rubber tires and faulty brakes up over the mountain passes. And if the truck didn't break down, the road was likely to, washed away by flooding or buried under a thundering rockfall. Today we accept the importance of the trucking industry to the economic well-being of British Columbia. But those early truckers were the ones who paved the way, risking their loads, and sometimes their lives, to navigate the rugged goat trails that passed for roads in the early days.

Following World War II trucking passed out of its pioneer phase into a period of consolidation and growth. A coherent system of paved highways reached out to the farthest corners of the province. Vehicles became more reliable and more powerful. Trucks began to challenge, then surpass, the rail-

A modern 18-wheeler with many of the aerodynamic extras speeds through the Fraser Valley in 2012. Truck design has come a long way in one hundred years. David Nunuk photo

They don't make 'em like that any more—either the log, the truck or the driver. Frank White measures up against a king-sized Douglas fir log he hauled on a truck owned by Bill Schnare near Sardis, BC, 1937. Courtesy of Howard White

Men of Special Experience

"When I think of those very first truckers who were in on the start of the rural truck lines, they were larger than life. Guys like Herb Wareing, Bob Groat, Eric Fox, Jimmy Vanderspek. Herb Wareing was hauling freight to my dad in 1926–27–28. It always made our day when Herb showed up. Towards the end, I remember particularly the old man was sick and failing and had no money to pay for his COD shipments, but Herb would give him the goods anyway and trust him to come up with the money later. Herb always brought news from down the line or had a story to tell... I looked up to truckers. They were the only people who saw the country in those days. They were respected. People sought them out, wanted their opinions. They were men of special experience."
– Frank White, former driver

ways as the favoured means of transporting freight. The 1950s saw a proliferation of regional carriers around the province, companies such as Chapmans Freight Lines in Kelowna, Van-Kam Freightways in Kamloops, Millar and Brown in Cranbrook, Northern Freightways in Dawson Creek, Berry & Smith in Penticton. These companies, and others like them, rode the wave of postwar expansion that swept over British Columbia. During the 1960s and 1970s, through the process of merger and acquisition, a small number of large, Lower Mainland–based companies emerged. Public Freightways was one; CP Transport, Johnston Terminals and Arrow Transport were others. This period of growth and realignment culminated with the end of federal economic regulation during the 1980s and provincial deregulation in the 1990s. During those years the industry experienced a bit of a shakedown as some companies survived and prospered in the newly competitive environment while others did not.

Left: This 1963 Kenworth was a workhorse in the Chapmans Freight Lines stable. Chapmans was one of the main companies hauling between the coast and Prince George into the 1990s. Courtesy of Bruce Shantz

Below: Neither of these pre-World War I era vehicles even had a cab for the driver who had to sit out exposed to the elements. The truck at the bottom is being delivered by rail.

Below: Royal BC Museum, BC Archives, I-60944. Harry Coutts photo; bottom: Royal BC Museum, BC Archives, D-03693

Jack Vleeming prepares to set off on his nightly run to Prince George for Clark Freightways, hauling a 53-foot refrigerated trailer. David Nunuk photo

Opposite: Highway 1 through the Fraser and Thompson canyons has been a main truck route to the Interior since it opened in 1927. David Nunuk photo

A Modern Trucker

Jack Vleeming started driving in his native Alberta when he was eighteen years old. At age sixty-eight he's been at it for fifty years and he's never really wanted to do anything else. His son is a driver and he has a brother in the industry as well, so whatever the attraction is, it runs in the family. Jack has driven almost every highway in the province, and south into the US; for many years he has been a lease operator with Clark Freightways.

Jack's regular run takes him overnight from Clark's warehouse in Coquitlam through the Fraser Canyon and up the Cariboo Highway to Prince George. Lately he's been driving his brand new Volvo hauling a sixteen-metre (fifty-three-foot) reefer van filled with a wide variety of temperature-controlled freight. The new vehicle has an automatic transmission and as it sweeps up a long grade Jack explains how he doesn't miss having to heave a pair of manual gearshifts down through the changes. Modern cab design and engine controls have taken much of the discomfort out of driving, but it is still a job that requires intense concentration as the driver keeps a constant watch on everything that is going on. Sitting in the heated cab as the kilometres tick by, a passenger can forget that there are many tons of freight riding along behind, but the driver cannot.

On this particular night the snow-capped peaks are sparkling in the moonlight as Jack cruises north through the canyon. There is a bit of fog as he crests the top of Jackass Mountain and around Williams Lake the snow falls for an hour or so but all in all the road is clear. Just south of Quesnel, where he makes a regular stop to drop off some way freight, Jack passes a tandem trailer outfit from another company that is pulled over on the opposite side of the road, its rear van crumpled as if it has collapsed in the middle. It's not clear what happened but Jack reckons that nowadays he sees a serious accident almost every trip, and compares it ruefully to his younger days, when one fatality in a year was rare. For Jack, the roads are getting more crowded and the industry more competitive but he continues to drive according to his credo: "Never be in a hurry." He believes that impatience and fatigue cause most accidents.

Jack makes the haul to Prince George two to three times a week. He leaves the Lower Mainland between ten and eleven most nights and if all goes well, which it usually does, he rolls into Prince George between eight and nine the next morning. Dumping his trailer, Jack curls up in the back of the cab for some shut-eye. He returns to the road at dinnertime and arrives back at the Coquitlam warehouse in the early hours of the morning, where he'll catch a few hours' sleep in the truck before heading home. Then, unless he has a day or two off, he will be back out on the road that night.

Jack agrees it is not a life that appeals to everyone, but he has always liked the independence, the challenge and the camaraderie, as well as the knowledge that he belongs to a group of professionals doing important work.

The BC trucking industry

- carries seventy percent of all freight, by value;
- employs close to 60,000 people;
- consists of more than 23,000 registered companies, the majority of them small to medium-sized businesses;
- represents 2.6 percent of BC's gross domestic product, which is a higher share than coal mining, pulp and paper, or agriculture;
- utilizes 24,000 kilometres (15,000 miles) of paved highways in the province and another 19,000 kilometres (12,000 miles) of unpaved roads;
- pays annual taxes and fees of $40,635 for a typical five-axle tractor and dry-van semi-trailer combination, including fuel taxes, licence fees, income tax and so on.

Today, more than fifteen years after deregulation, the motor freight industry continues to play its essential role in the national and provincial economy. Over ninety percent of the goods moved within Canada depend on truck transportation, either solely or in partnership with air, rail or marine shipments. Trucks provide Canadians with the necessities of their lives, whether that means food for the dinner table, raw materials for mills and factories, or consumer goods for store shelves. Canada-wide, trucking is a multi-billion-dollar industry. In 2008 trucking employed more than 415,000 full-time workers, of whom more than 270,000 were drivers. Some were women but the vast majority were men, and truck driving was the second-leading male occupation in the country at the time. As well, the industry employed tens of thousands more people in related occupations, such as truck, trailer and parts manufacturing, sales, maintenance and back office support. As the leading employer in the transportation sector, trucking employed more than twice as many people in Canada as air and rail combined.

In British Columbia, the story is the same. According to Statistics Canada, for-hire trucking was a $1.88 billion industry in the province in 2009. More impressively, that figure is probably understated by as much as half because StatsCan does not include private trucks in its data. Outside of service industries such as health care, education and public administration, only forestry and the oil and gas industry contribute more to the provincial GDP. There are about 23,000 trucking companies active in BC, the majority of which are small, owner-operator-run businesses with five trucks or less. Large companies, those with a fleet size of twenty-one or more vehicles, account for just three percent of the total.

Despite the competitive nature of the industry, the number of trucks at work in the province increased substantially between 2000 and 2007, from 46,427 medium- and heavy-duty trucks in 2000 to

Container cranes light up the night sky at the Deltaport container terminal at Roberts Bank.

David Nunuk photo

Barometer of the Economy

"The trucking industry is a great barometer of the economy. The trucking industry hauls inventory. When the economy starts to go into recession, the trucking industry feels it pretty well right away because that is when the factories and the warehouses stop shipping. Production goes down and the impact is pretty quick. And vice versa. When things pick up, you are usually short of equipment because you've taken trucks off the road because business has gone down. And now all of sudden production has picked up and the requirement for hauling freight has increased."
— *Shub Bawa, Marpole Transport*

56,043 seven years later. Due to the impact of the worldwide economic downturn that began in 2008 the trend has reversed, but judging by past experience the reversal will be temporary. It is fair to say that in the long term trucking is a growth industry.

Canada's economy is heavily dependent on trade, especially with the United States. In 2010 trade with the US totalled more than $500 billion. And almost sixty percent of that trade was carried by truck. This volume declined due to the economic slowdown, but trucking continues to be the dominant player in cross-border transportation. A truck crosses the US–Canada border every few seconds. Here in BC, the Pacific Highway crossing in Surrey is the fourth-busiest commercial crossing in Canada in terms of truck traffic volume. (Huntingdon in Abbotsford is the fourteenth busiest.) Even in

international trade, where marine and air transportation are important, trucks carry twenty-two percent of the volume through their intermodal connections with rail and the ports in the Lower Mainland and at Prince Rupert. At some point in the delivery chain, trucks transport goods making up just over half of the value of Canada's trade with the world.

A Coca-Cola truck tackles the Sea-to-Sky Highway on a run to Squamish. Coca-Cola is an example of a manufacturer that prefers to operate its own private fleet of vehicles, which are moving billboards for its product.
David Nunuk photo

The trucking industry is traditionally comprised of three broad categories of carriers—for-hire motor carriers, private fleet operators and owner-operators—though the differences between them are less clear-cut than they once were. For-hire carriers are companies whose business it is to haul freight for remuneration. Private trucking is performed by companies that have their own fleets of vehicles for transporting their goods; that is, their principal business is not trucking. Private carriers own the freight they are carrying; for-hire carriers do not. Coca-Cola, for example, produces and delivers its own product in its own trucks. Another private arrangement is what is called third-party logistics (3PL), where

a carrier's services are contracted for one hundred percent of the load and the carrier works almost exclusively for one customer; for example, Martin-Brower of Canada Co. is the distributor of products to the McDonald's chain of restaurants. In this case the private carrier actually takes ownership of the freight for the duration of the haul. Owner-operators are for-hire carriers who own or lease their own equipment. There are somewhere in the neighbourhood of 100,000 owner-operators in Canada. Some may haul freight on their own account, obtaining cargo through brokers on a trip-by-trip basis; these operators are sometimes called independent truckers. Others may have long-term relationships with one or more particular shippers or work directly for for-hire trucking companies.

When it comes to general freight hauling, an important distinction is made between truckload (TL) carriers and less-than-truckload (LTL) carriers. Companies tend to specialize in one or the other. LTL carriers perform pickup services and then consolidate multiple shipments destined for various consignees in one truck. They require terminals where freight picked up from local customers is transferred to longer-haul vehicles for outbound delivery, and vice versa, and may offer a scheduled service along fixed routes. Truckload carriers generally pick up a full trailer from one shipper, a load destined to one consignee for final delivery. Shipments occupy entire trucks and move from shipper to destination

Above: Cold Star Freight Systems is a Victoria-based company specializing in the delivery of refrigerated products between Vancouver Island and the Lower Mainland. Here trucks are loading up at the company warehouse.

David Nunuk photo

17

Above: Hauling wood chips is a specialized business in BC. When the product arrives at this depot, the entire truck-trailer unit is hoisted on a hydraulic lift to dump the chips into silos. The Exploration Place, Wally West Collection

Right: A logging truck crosses a trestle bridge on Vancouver Island in 1949. Trucks had been proving their usefulness to the forest industry since the 1920s. UBC Library, Rare Books and Special Collections, MacMillan Bloedel Ltd. fonds, BC 1930/37/6

without any need for transhipment through terminals. TL service is on demand and does not follow a particular schedule (though in this just-in-time era, delivery at a pre-arranged time is common and often critical).

Of course there are many more kinds of carriers if they are categorized by types of freight. The range of goods carried by today's fleet of high-performance vehicles is stunning in its variety. Van trailers carry general consumer goods to stock the shelves of stores and supermarkets across the province. Auto haulers use double-decker trailers to transport new automobiles from the manufacturer to the dealer. Refrigerated vans ("reefers") carry meat, fruit and vegetables, delivered just in time to be available fresh for consumers. Bulk carriers haul a range of commodities both liquid and dry that have to be blown, poured or shovelled into place—petroleum, wood chips, cement, sulphur, gravel, chemicals of different kinds; the list is endless. Furniture movers shift customers' belongings across the city and across the continent, while logging trucks negotiate the perilous mountain roads of the backcountry, hauling logs from the most remote cut sites. Dump trucks carry dirt and gravel; flat decks haul the heavy machinery and large construction materials that keep the province building. It is difficult to wrap one's mind around the diversity that the single term "trucking" embodies.

What Is a Truck?

A truck generally means a motor vehicle with six or more tires and with a gross vehicle weight (GVW) of at least 4,500 kilograms (about 10,000 pounds) that is primarily involved in the movement of goods. This excludes pickups and small vans. The most familiar trucks that the general public encounters on the road are the large tractor-trailer combinations used for hauling freight long distances, straight trucks of varying sizes for local pickup and delivery, tankers carrying bulk fuels and other liquid cargo, and tractors hauling containers from the port or the rail yard. Away from the highway, trucks are just as important in farming and the natural resource industries. There were 749,000 trucks in Canada in 2010, of which almost thirty percent were tractor-trailers; the rest were the straight trucks that predominate in city streets.

Trucking is a highly competitive business. And it is reasonably easy for someone to get into the industry, especially since the economic deregulation that began to occur across North America during the 1980s. The infrastructure, in the form of roads and bridges, is already provided. The owner simply has to purchase a truck, or hire an owner-operator with his or her own truck, and obtain a National Safety Code certificate (the NSC establishes minimum safety standards for vehicles and drivers). As Paul Landry, the first full-time president of the BC Trucking Association, once put it, "it is a lot more difficult to set up a mobile hot dog stand than to start a trucking company."

The result has been high levels of competition, small profit margins and constant innovation. Trucking is especially sensitive to the ups and downs of the economy as a whole and reacts quickly to the pressures of supply and demand. When the economy slows so does overall production, and the demand for truck services follows suit. If you want to know where the economy is headed, keep your eye on the trucking industry.

Opposite: This modern rig is hauling a container up the Coquihalla Highway.

David Nunuk photo

This detail decorates the hood of a 1963 Mack B-61 diesel, a favourite model with long-haul drivers. Mack manufactured the B series from 1953 to 1966. Kevin Oke photo

Trucks have come a long way since the first Model A Fords with jerry-rigged boxes on the back began hauling furniture and fresh produce around the streets of BC's towns and cities. By the time the coast obtained its first highway connection to the Interior in the 1920s, vehicles featured pneumatic tires, four-speed transmissions, a load capacity of five tons and other improvements. As the road system spread to every corner of the province, trucks increased steadily in size and comfort. Today's giant rigs are technological marvels, incorporating the latest in computerized drive management and environmentally friendly design. During the 1930s it took four days to drive to the Okanagan from the coast. Modern trucks now provide overnight freight service to most of the province's major centres. Not only do they travel at four times the speed, they can do so using half the amount of fuel, thanks to aerodynamic cabs and trailers, high-performance diesel engines and on-board computerized performance systems that monitor everything from engine idling to vehicle speed.

The story of the achievements of this dynamic industry, which has made such a major contribution to the growth and integration of British Columbia, is the subject of this book.

TIMELINE OF INDUSTRY MILESTONES

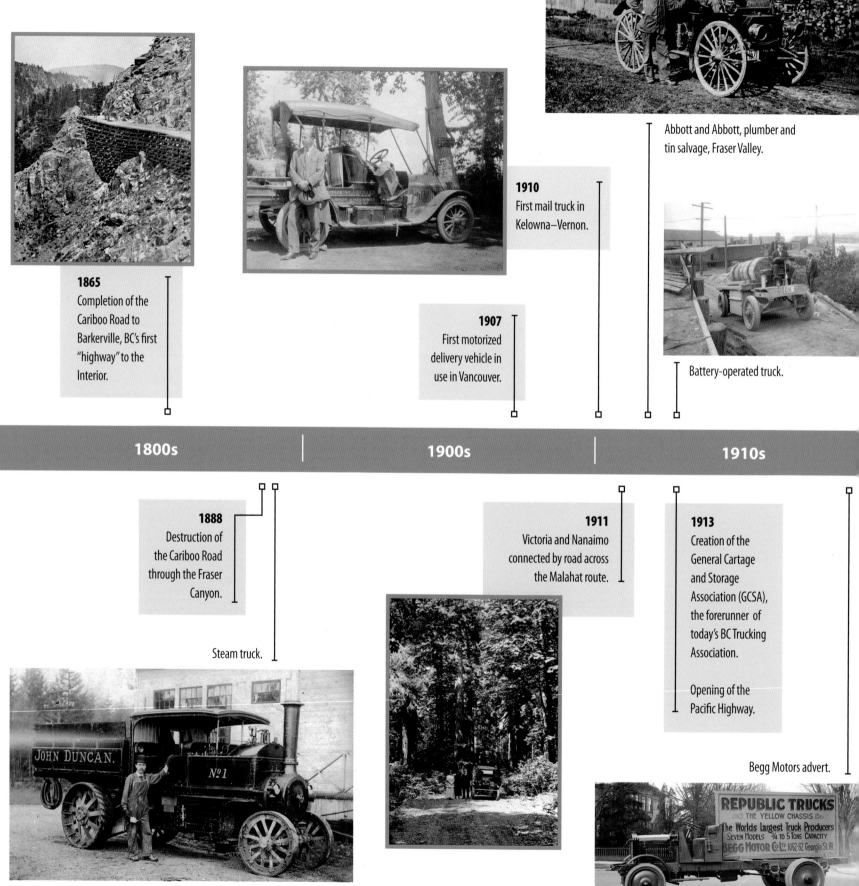

Abbott and Abbott, plumber and tin salvage, Fraser Valley.

1910
First mail truck in Kelowna–Vernon.

1907
First motorized delivery vehicle in use in Vancouver.

1865
Completion of the Cariboo Road to Barkerville, BC's first "highway" to the Interior.

Battery-operated truck.

1800s   1900s   1910s

1888
Destruction of the Cariboo Road through the Fraser Canyon.

Steam truck.

1911
Victoria and Nanaimo connected by road across the Malahat route.

1913
Creation of the General Cartage and Storage Association (GCSA), the forerunner of today's BC Trucking Association.

Opening of the Pacific Highway.

Begg Motors advert.

JOHN DUNCAN. No 1

REPUBLIC TRUCKS
THE YELLOW CHASSIS
The Worlds Largest Truck Producers
SEVEN MODELS   ¾ TO 5 TONS CAPACITY
BEGG MOTOR Co Ltd 1062-82 Georgia St. W.

Heavy hauling.

Red Cross supplies.

1920
Hayes-Anderson Motor Co. established in Vancouver. (Closed in 1975.)

1930
The GCSA becomes the Commercial Motor Vehicle Owners' Association (CMVOA).

Shell oil tanker.

1940
Opening of the Big Bend Highway between Revelstoke and Golden.

BC government establishes the Motor Carrier Branch to regulate the industry.

Some carriers form the Automotive Transport Association (ATA).

1949
Hope–Princeton Highway opens.

1920s   1930s   1940s

1927
Fraser Canyon Highway reopens, once again connecting the Lower Mainland to the Interior.

1934
The CMVOA is replaced by the Motor Carriers' Association (MCA).

Okanagan apple freighting.

1942
Alaska Highway opens.

1946
The ATA and the MCA merge to form the Automotive Transport Association of British Columbia (ATABC).

1947
BC government removes tolls from the Fraser Canyon route.

Dominion Tire truck in World War I victory celebration, Vancouver.

Plate glass carrier.

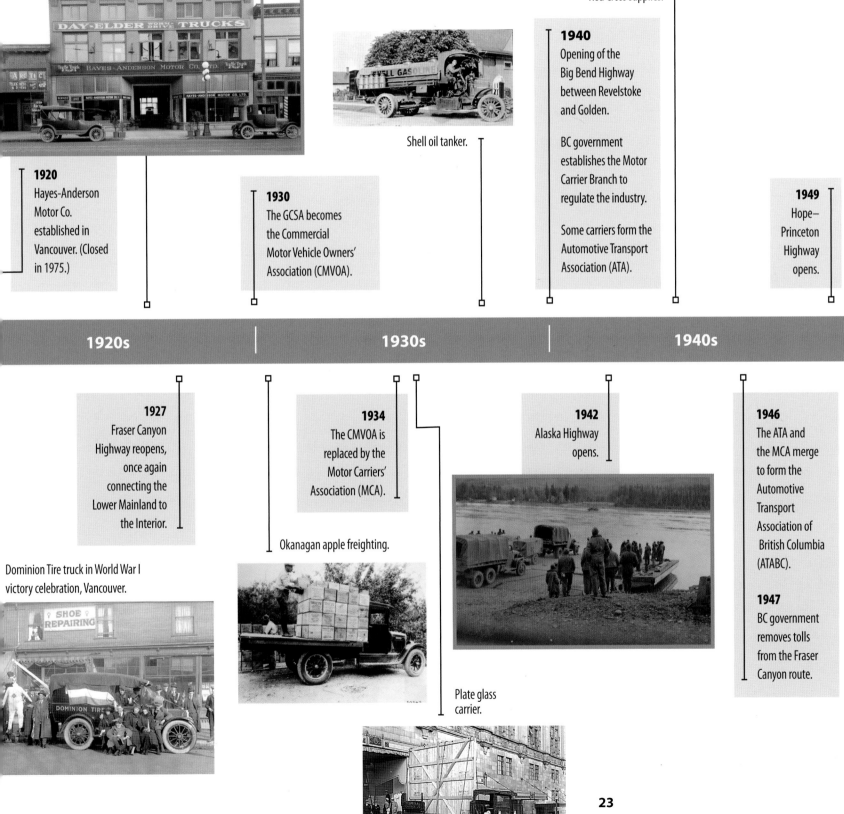

Truck accident.

Asbestos truck, Cassiar.

1950
National rail strike provides opportunity for trucking industry to prove its worth to the national economy.

1955
Chilcotin Highway is extended to Bella Coola.

Toms Brothers, Port Alberni.

1973
The new Motor Carrier Commission takes over industry regulation from the Public Utilities Commission.

1950s   1960s   1970s

1952
Hart Highway opens between Prince George and Dawson Creek.

1962
Official opening of the Trans-Canada Highway at Rogers Pass.

New Alexandra Bridge allows longer rigs on the Fraser Canyon route.

Vancouver–Blaine Freeway completed.

Picking up freight, Port of Vancouver.

1978
ATABC becomes the BC Motor Transport Association (BCMTA).

A Jersey Farms delivery horse meets the future, an electric dairy truck.

Hayes HDX hauling for MacMillan Bloedel near Port Alberni.

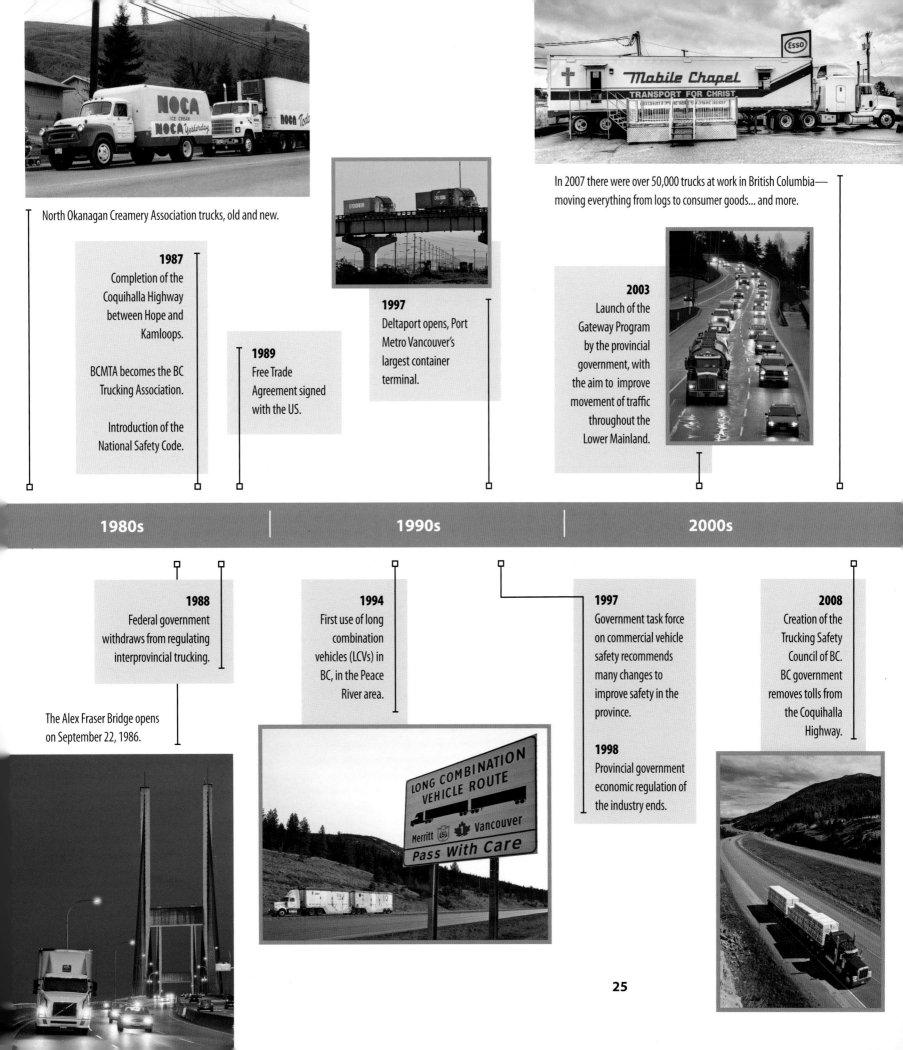

North Okanagan Creamery Association trucks, old and new.

In 2007 there were over 50,000 trucks at work in British Columbia—moving everything from logs to consumer goods... and more.

1987
Completion of the Coquihalla Highway between Hope and Kamloops.

BCMTA becomes the BC Trucking Association.

Introduction of the National Safety Code.

1989
Free Trade Agreement signed with the US.

1997
Deltaport opens, Port Metro Vancouver's largest container terminal.

2003
Launch of the Gateway Program by the provincial government, with the aim to improve movement of traffic throughout the Lower Mainland.

1980s | 1990s | 2000s

1988
Federal government withdraws from regulating interprovincial trucking.

The Alex Fraser Bridge opens on September 22, 1986.

1994
First use of long combination vehicles (LCVs) in BC, in the Peace River area.

1997
Government task force on commercial vehicle safety recommends many changes to improve safety in the province.

1998
Provincial government economic regulation of the industry ends.

2008
Creation of the Trucking Safety Council of BC. BC government removes tolls from the Coquihalla Highway.

25

From Wagon Roads to Highways

The story of trucking begins with the history of roads. Until a network of useable roads spread up the river valleys and across the mountain passes of the BC interior, the trucking of freight was limited to urban areas, which in early-twentieth-century British Columbia meant the Lower Mainland and southern Vancouver Island. As roads were built, truckers used them to haul freight to the distant corners of the province.

Opposite: The Cariboo Road through the Fraser Canyon was the first "highway" in BC. This section across China Bar Bluff shows the cribbing needed to support the road.

Left: A much newer road to the Interior is the Coquihalla Highway between Hope and Kamloops, completed in 1987.

Royal BC Museum, BC Archives, A-03867, Frederick Dally photo; David Nunuk photo

At the same time, the development of new trucking technologies pushed at the limits of road capacity, requiring improved thoroughfares to accommodate the ever larger and more powerful vehicles.

In the early years of the twentieth century, however, when motorized vehicles were replacing the horse-drawn wagon as the principal means of transporting goods, trucking in British Columbia was challenged by a road network that had not changed since the days of gold dust and mule trains. Discouraged by the mountainous topography of the Interior, road builders had not expanded their activities much beyond the main population centres in the southwest corner of the province. A notable exception was the Cariboo Road, the great accomplishment of pioneer road building in British Columbia.

With the discovery of gold in the gravel shoals of the Fraser Canyon in 1858 and then in the creeks of the Cariboo, Governor James Douglas recognized the need for a wagon road to connect gold camps of the Interior to the coast. Construction began in 1862 at Yale, the head of steamboat navigation; three years later the road arrived at Barkerville, 492 kilometres (306 miles) to the north. Immediately the roadway filled with a variety of freight vehicles—at least during the summer months—everything from hand-pushed wheelbarrows loaded with mining gear to ox-drawn freight wagons. Even camels were used as pack animals, but only briefly: the rocky surface turned out to be too hard on their feet.

One experimental freight vehicle more directly linked to trucks was the Thomson Road Steamer, designed in Scotland and brought in to haul freight on the Cariboo Road in 1871. Featuring India-rubber tires and a huge boiler, this tractor-like vehicle set off from Yale on its inaugural trip pulling six tons of

27

The Thomson Road Steamer was one of the odder vehicles to drive the Cariboo Road. It was meant to replace horse-drawn wagons but the experiment was a failure. Of the six steamers imported from England, one remained in the province and was used to haul logs in what is now Kitsilano. Innovators did not stop trying to use steam vehicles on the road, however.

Right: A steam tractor hauls a couple of wagons on what looks like a construction job in the early 1900s.

Top: Royal BC Museum, BC Archives A-07822; right: Royal BC Museum, BC Archives D-07724

freight, but after three days the cumbersome behemoth had only reached Jackass Mountain, a distance of fifty kilometres (thirty-one miles), and the experiment was declared a failure.

Freight wagons shared the road with stagecoaches of the famed BX Line. The line was founded by Francis J. Barnard, who had come west from his native Quebec to join the gold rush. Disappointed as a prospector, he began carrying mail between Yale and Barkerville; the business evolved into Barnard's Express and Stage Line (the "BX"), a fleet of stagecoaches specializing in the transport of passengers, gold, mail and express freight. (In the winter, sleighs replaced the coaches.) Barnard boasted that he owned the longest stagecoach run in North America and he probably did. His company, later called the BC Express Company, remained in business until 1915, which is about the time the earliest motorized vehicles began to appear on the scene.

Following the completion of the Cariboo Road, rough wagon roads were constructed in haphazard fashion to reach gold strikes in different parts of the Interior or to link pioneer communities. But the arrival of the transcontinental railway in 1885 overshadowed road building altogether: rail seemed to offer the promise of the future, not roads. In fact, the construction of the Canadian Pacific Railway through the Fraser Canyon actually destroyed the section of the Cariboo Road between Yale and Spences Bridge. Andrew Onderdonk, the engineer in charge of CPR construction through the canyon, had instructions to keep the wagon road open, but inevitably blasting for the rail line blew apart great sections of the original route and buried other parts under tons of rock and dirt. Whatever remained of the roadbed and trestles was obliterated further by the destructive flooding of 1894 and the construction of the Canadian Northern Pacific Railway, a second rail line that was pushed through the Fraser Canyon prior to World War I. According to transportation historian R.G. Harvey, the government maintained a pretense that the road still existed, at least until 1910, but actually from 1888 the interior of the province was cut off from the coast so far as road traffic was concerned.

Once motor vehicles began to appear, the only way to drive between the lower Fraser Valley and BC's central interior was to dip south of the border. Vehicles heading from Vancouver to the US border travelled along Kingsway to New Westminster, crossed the Fraser River on the dual car and train bridge

Left: A car and a freight wagon meet on the Cariboo Road in 1910. Note that the car is driving on the left side of the road, which was the practice in BC until January 1, 1922, when traffic switched over. Royal BC Museum, BC Archives I-58408

Below: This is the official opening of the dual car and railway bridge across the Fraser River at New Westminster on July 23, 1904. Built at a cost of $1 million, it provided cars access to the valley, and the Great Northern Railway access to the city. City of Vancouver Archives M-2-71

Left: A worker spreads gravel on the roadbed of the Island Highway south of Nanaimo in 1921. By 1930 the highway reached all the way from Victoria to Campbell River.

Royal BC Museum, BC Archives A-07285

Below: This was the Customs House at the US border on the Pacific Highway from 1913 to 1923. Royal BC Museum, BC Archives D-02556

Opposite: Another dual rail/car bridge was the first Second Narrows Bridge across Burrard Inlet in Vancouver, shown here in June 1926, eight months after it opened. The span had two lanes for automobile traffic, divided by a centre rail line.

Vancouver Public Library 6462, Leonard Frank photo

31

The highway in the Fraser Canyon passes through seven tunnels, including the 286-metre-long Yale Tunnel. The tunnel was completed in 1963 as part of the Trans-Canada Highway upgrade project.

David Nunuk photo

that had opened there in 1904 and followed the Pacific Highway, which opened in July 1913 and was paved ten years later, to the border. Through the Fraser Valley the Yale Road followed the south side of the river, while the Dewdney Trunk Road was the main artery on the north side. On Vancouver Island a gravel road across the Malahat route connected Victoria to Nanaimo in 1911; it was extended all the way to Campbell River by 1930.

As motor cars began to appear in increasing numbers in BC, their owners began to lobby government for improved roads. In 1911 a group of automotive enthusiasts from New Westminster formed the Canadian Highway Association for the purpose of promoting the construction of a transcontinental motorway from Vancouver Island to Halifax. The following year the group held a rally at Alberni where it unveiled an optimistic road sign marked "Canadian Highway" with an arrow pointing eastward. To further promote its objective of better roads, the CHA offered a gold medal to the first motorist to succeed in driving across Canada. It would be thirty-four years before anyone actually made the drive and claimed the medal, but obviously the arrival of "car culture" was putting pressure on governments to do something about the sorry state of the roads in the country and in the province.

In British Columbia there was a significant amount of pre-war road building going on with the energetic support of the first minister of the new department of public works, Thomas "Good Roads" Taylor. Helped along by the pre-war economic boom, Taylor managed to double the number of roads in the province during the six years he served as minister (1908–1914). Many of these thoroughfares were in the Interior, where a network of trunk

Above: Thomas "Good Roads" Taylor, minister of public works in the government of Richard McBride, was an important supporter of road building in the province. Royal BC Museum, BC Archives, Image A-02489

Top left: A crew paves West Sixteenth Avenue in Vancouver in 1929. For many years this street was the boundary of the city. Everything to the south as far as the Fraser River was a separate municipality, South Vancouver. On January 1, 1929, the two communities merged. Leonard Frank photo, Vancouver Public Library 11534

Left: A crowd gathers at Alberni on May 4, 1912, to kick off a campaign for a "Canadian Highway." Jewish Museum and Archives of BC, LF.38816, Leonard Frank photo

roads was rapidly linking communities to each other. Despite the sacrifice of its southern section to the railway builders, the Cariboo Road still ran from Spences Bridge north as far as Quesnel, and then on to Prince George. Salmon Arm was connected by a wagon road to Armstrong and Vernon, and according to R.G. Harvey one of the best roads in the province ran along the west side of Okanagan Lake from Penticton to near Kelowna, though even it was pockmarked by potholes and made dangerous by tortuous curves. "I purchased a car this fall," complained a local rancher in a letter to the minister of public works, "and now I find it a dangerous article to run and rather wish someone else had it."

The road running east from Kamloops ended at Revelstoke. The Selkirk Mountains remained a barrier to road builders for many years, and the only way to reach Golden was to ship a motor vehicle on a CPR flatcar. On the eastern side of the mountains a road ran south from Golden to Cranbrook, where it connected with a route to Alberta via the Crowsnest Pass. On July 11, 1911, the first car driven through the pass arrived in Cranbrook from Calgary; it was a Tudhope-Everitt made by the Orillia-based Tudhope Motor Co. Every community had a few venturesome, and wealthy, business leaders—mill owners, bankers and merchants—who were the owners of the first cars and lobbied the government on behalf of more roads. In 1909 there were only 504 motor vehicles in the province, but by the outbreak of the war in 1914 that number had risen to 6,688 including trucks, and the number was doubling every year.

As the road network expanded, bridges were built to provide vehicle access to many of the small towns of the Interior. This bridge is under construction at Horsefly, east of Williams Lake, in about 1927. Quesnel & District Museum and Archives, P2003.2.643

Above: A small roadblock stalls the "pathfinding car" trying to find a useable overland route from Edmonton to the coast, via Jasper and Kamloops, in 1922. Surprisingly, they made it, arriving in Victoria after seventeen days.

Left: The first car arrives in Hazelton in August, 1911, claiming a thousand-dollar reward.

Columbia Basin Institute of Regional History; Royal BC Museum, BC Archives B-01340

Right: A couple of men load the tobacco harvest in a field near Kelowna, c. 1919. Farmers were quick to adapt the early trucks to agricultural purposes.

Below: In urban areas the earliest trucks were delivery vans like this one, a Packard, delivering ice and coal in Vancouver in 1917.

Kelowna Public Archives 3676; City of Vancouver Archives, CVA A17630, Stuart Thomson photo

Left: The Carswell motion picture truck, splashed with advertisements from local businesses, sits outside the Vernon movie house, c. 1922. The movie bill shows that "Grandma's Boy" starring Harold Lloyd is showing.

Below: A six-wheel Moreland transport truck arrives in Vancouver in 1925 as part of a publicity tour. Moreland was a California-based manufacturer of heavy-duty vehicles and this TX6 model was the first six-wheeler on the road.

Vernon Museum & Archives, No. 95; City of Vancouver Archives, CVA 1477-682, W.J. Moore photo

Below: A couple of vehicles make their way up the Canyon Highway between Spuzzum and Lytton during the 1930s.

Bottom left: A Reo truck, owned by George Brooks, was pinned by a falling rock at Nine Mile Point in the canyon. The passenger was unhurt.

Bottom right: This rock slide near Hope, c. 1940, held up traffic for three days before it was cleared.

Royal BC Museum, BC Archives, A-04683; Courtesy of Rod Parkinson; Quesnel & District Museum and Archives P1997.20.1

By 1925 British Columbia had 28,670 kilometres (17,800 miles) of roads, a significant amount even if you ignored the fact that only 255 kilometres (160 miles) were hard surfaced and fully 16,000 kilometres (10,000 miles) were officially defined as "dirt trails." The most common road surface was loose gravel; roadbeds were narrow and fell away in precipitous drops; snow removal was almost non-existent. In the Interior at least, driving was left to the adventurer, not the motorist. And in the post-war economic climate, the government was no longer doing much to improve the situation. During 1925, for example, the province added a mere thirty-five kilometres (twenty-two miles) of hard-surfaced road, mostly in the Lower Mainland—which was a clear indication of the low priority road building enjoyed.

Nonetheless, and most significantly for long-haul trucking, the provincial government of the day decided it was time to re-establish a road connection between the coast and the Interior by reopening the Fraser Canyon route. Work began in 1924 and on May 24, 1927, the Fraser Canyon Highway officially opened. For the next twenty years, the story of long-haul trucking in British Columbia was the story of the Canyon Highway. The road, which was initially only open from the beginning of May to the middle of November, was narrow, gravel surfaced (asphalt paving did not begin along the Canyon Highway until the mid-1930s) and often closed due to washouts, slides and snowstorms in the late spring and early autumn. Given the perils of driving the route, it is not surprising that few vehicles used it. The government collected tolls at a small shack at Spuzzum and in 1928, the second year the highway was open, only eighty-one vehicles passed through in August, the most active month, and a mere fifteen in November, just before it closed for the season. By 1933 traffic varied from a daily low of seventeen trucks in April to a high of 167 in August. Truckers liked to take the road at night when car traffic was light but it was harder to see the rock slides and washouts that might have occurred since the last time they travelled the canyon. Andy Craig, a pioneer trucker who later wrote a history of the industry's early years, described how he used to keep a spotlight aimed at the edge of the road "because it had a nasty habit of falling into the Fraser River without warning." Craig also said that "we seldom made a trip [through the canyon] without finding some unlucky soul who had hit a rock slide, or gone over the bank, or broken through an old bridge." On one trip in 1936 the road was washed out by a huge rock slide. For two days stranded drivers worked to make a rough track across the slide and eventually the convoy of trucks got moving again.

The toll on the Fraser Canyon route was two dollars per ton on the gross weight of truck and cargo, which was not an insignificant sum in the middle of the Depression. As a result, truckers went out of their way to avoid paying it. Vehicles were weighed on a wooden platform sitting on four scales. Craig tells of how he and his fellow drivers would haul up onto the platform, then apply their brakes suddenly in an attempt to shift the platform off the scales. When this happened the toll takers just charged them at their declared weight, and the drivers saved a few dollars. The tolls were a constant grievance with truckers, who resented having their earnings depleted. Ostensibly the government applied the toll to pay for the highway but many drivers believed it was imposed as a favour to the railways to discourage freight movement by road. "If this financial tribute is for the maintenance of the Fraser Canyon section of the Trans-Canada Highway," opined the editors of *Motor Carrier* magazine, "why is it that tolls are not collected in similar fashion on every section of highway in the Province?" Despite such grumblings from the industry, tolls were collected until the booth, which moved to Yale in 1938, closed in 1947.

Beyond the canyon there were different routes for trucks to follow in these early days. At Lytton they might continue on up the Fraser to Lillooet and into the Bridge River country. At Spences Bridge trucks veered southeast toward Merritt and on to Princeton and the south Okanagan. Trucks heading toward Revelstoke and the north Okanagan continued to Cache Creek before turning east for Kamloops. The rest kept going north up the old Cariboo Road past Clinton and on to 100 Mile House, Williams Lake, Quesnel and Prince George. Beyond Prince George it was what Andy Craig called "pioneer freighting at its damndest." The gumbo was often so deep trucks would sink up to their chassis and had to be hauled out with block and tackle tied to the nearest tree. "Those roads by Vanderhoof and the Fort [St. James] were the worst I had experienced," he recalled, and that was saying a lot.

Top: This modified pickup truck is stuck in a
mud hole on the corduroy road to Ootsa Lake
south of Burns Lake in 1922.

Right: City streets were kept in better repair.
Here a crew is oiling a street in Prince George
to keep down the dust.

Bottom right: Between the wars, many interior
roads were little better than dirt tracks.

Royal BC Museum, BC Archives I-58793, Frank Swannell
photo; The Exploration Place; Quesnel & District Museum
and Archives P1986.13.1

Meanwhile, in the rural Fraser Valley, where a network of roads connected the various communities, one of the main uses for trucks in the interwar period was to haul milk from farms to the milk plant for processing and bottling. BC Electric had been operating an interurban tram line from Vancouver out to Chilliwack since the autumn of 1910. The Fraser Valley line was a great success, hauling milk and other produce from area farms on three daily trains into New Westminster and Vancouver—not to mention passengers who could make the 102-kilometre (63-mile) trip for a three-dollar return fare. Every station, and there were more than fifty of them, had a milk platform where farmers left their filled cans in the morning and picked up the empties in the afternoon.

At its height the milk train hauled ten baggage cars devoted almost exclusively to the dairy business. During the Depression, however, truckers began to challenge BC Electric's hold on the milk run. "All the milk had been shipped by the BC Electric trams going into Vancouver," explained Frank White, who began carrying milk from Abbotsford into Vancouver on a daily route in 1932. "But truckers could sneak in with their trucks and pick up right on the farms, and haul the milk into town cheaper than the BC Electric because they could haul freight back. So right in the middle of the Depression was this opportunity and trucking lines sprouted up all over the place. First they were hauling milk and then they were hauling everything." Another of these drivers was Charlie Siebold, who

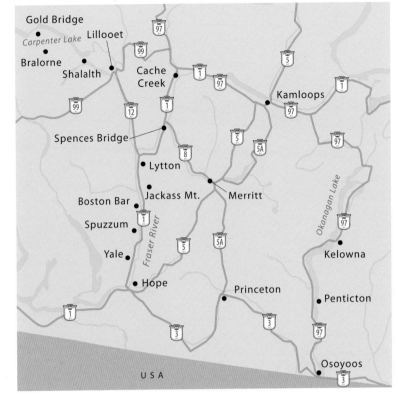

hauled milk in his BC-made Hayes truck during the 1930s. Each farmer had a stand out by the roadside where they put the filled cans. Siebold came by twice a day; he picked up the cans, drove them to the plant in New Westminster, offloaded the full cans and picked up the empties, then repeated his route of about twenty-four farms in the afternoon. By 1939 competition from truckers had helped convince BC Electric to get out of the milk-hauling business altogether.

Hauling milk from Fraser Valley farms into Greater Vancouver was good business for truckers between the wars. This photograph shows the first truck used for the purpose, owned by A. Edmondson, at Chilliwack c. 1910. Royal BC Museum, BC Archives D-01080

Above: In the Fraser Valley, farmers left their milk in cans out by the road. Truckers loaded the cans, delivered them to the dairy and returned with the empties, all in a day's work.

Right: Hauling milk was good business in the Okanagan as well. This truck belonged to the Okanagan Valley Co-operative Creamery Association, c. 1912.

Vancouver Public Library 81072A, Artray photo;
Vernon Museum & Archives, No. 903

Hauling Milk in the Depression

"There were no paved roads in the valley to speak of except the Pacific Highway and we'd come rolling down that. No Pattullo Bridge yet and you'd have to come across the river on the old railway bridge at New Westminster. It was the only bridge from the valley and it'd just take one line of trucks at a time. Creep up the hill and over to Kingsway and into Vancouver. Those little '32 Fords we were driving were only four-cylinder jobs, but we hauled five and six tons on them at times. Crawling back and forth, you'd just stumble along, gearing up and gearing down all the time."
— Frank White

The 1940s saw the completion of three crucial links in the highway chain. Since 1927 it had been possible to drive west into BC from Alberta as far as Golden but there the road came to an abrupt halt. British Columbians waited expectantly for the road to be extended across the Selkirk Mountains via the Rogers Pass to Revelstoke, but nothing happened. The route over the pass was deemed impractical. Instead, the federal government, as partner in the construction plans, proposed to the province that together they build what came to be called the Big Bend Highway, a looping 305-kilometre (190-mile) stretch following the bend of the Columbia River north from Golden and then south again into Revelstoke. Built during the Depression as an unemployment relief project, the Big Bend took ten long years to complete. Construction was prolonged by the roughness of the terrain and the remoteness of the area, not to mention the state of the economy. Officially opened on June 29, 1940, it filled the last gap in the trans-provincial highway and made it possible to drive from Alberta to the coast entirely within BC for the first time.

Left: Construction of the Big Bend Highway went on all during the 1930s. Here the camp is being moved to the next site.

Above: On June 29, 1940, Premier Duff Pattullo cuts a ribbon at the Boat Encampment bridge to officially open the highway.

The fact that it was possible, however, did not mean that it was easy. The Big Bend was a narrow, extremely dusty gravel road, with steep drop-offs into the valley of the Columbia River below; it took an ordinary car seven hours to negotiate the trip. And heavy snowfall closed the road from November to May. A travel writer for the *Ottawa Citizen* called it "the loneliest road in North America." Understandably, truckers did not rush to use the new route.

The second link was a vital wartime project in the northeast corner of the province, the Alaska Highway. With the Japanese attack on the US naval base at Pearl Harbor at the end of 1941, the Americans became especially concerned about the security of Alaska, where they feared the Japanese might invade. The US received permission from Canada to build a highway from Alberta across the northeast corner of BC to Alaska via Dawson Creek and Fort St. John. The American military constructed the new road in just eight months. The engineer in charge of the project divided his men into fourteen groups and gave each one responsibility for a particular section of the road, meaning that crews pushed north and south from several spots along the route. On November 20, 1942, it was ready for military traffic. Canada had been promised that the road would become a useable peacetime highway, so even as the military began using it, civilian crews came north to improve it. Places like Dawson Creek and Fort St. John boomed with all the activity. But as the fear of Japanese invasion faded, so did the urgency to complete the project and the portion of the gravel highway that was turned over to Canada in April 1946, as per agreement, fell far short of the quality that had been promised. Still, it was a beginning. The inaccessible reaches of northeastern BC were now open to development, and trucking.

The third link completed the long-awaited southern route through the province. On November 2, 1949, the Hope–Princeton Highway opened

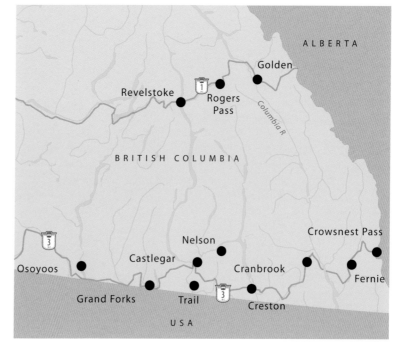

Above: A modern truck barrels down the BC section of the Alaska Highway.

Right: A flotilla of vehicles awaiting delivery to the Alaska Highway construction site in 1940.

David Nunuk photo; Columbia Basin Institute of Regional History

The Alexandra Bridge, though beautiful, was a bit of a bottleneck for truckers using the Fraser Canyon route to the Interior since it could only cope with vehicles of a certain size. This bridge was actually the second on the site. The original had been built in 1863 as part of the Cariboo Wagon Road but it was washed out in 1894. Erected in 1926, this second bridge was replaced in 1962 allowing larger truck configurations to use the Canyon. Vancouver Public Library 34138, Donovan Clemson photo

across Allison Pass. Motor vehicles could now reach the Interior without, in the words of the future highways minister Phil Gaglardi, "this blasted business of going through the United States to get from one part of British Columbia to another part." The completion of the Hope–Princeton was especially important for truckers. So long as traffic was confined to the Fraser Canyon route, trucks could not exceed nine metres (thirty feet), the maximum length that could manoeuvre through the Alexandra Bridge bottleneck north of Yale, and 13,500 kilograms (30,000 pounds) GVW. (According to Andy Craig, though, Ebert Lee drove a ten-and-a-half-metre—thirty-five-foot—semi-trailer through in 1941; at the time, it was the longest truck ever to make the trip.) As well, the old wooden bridges could not hold more weight; but as they were converted to steel, maximum weights went up to 18,000 kilograms (40,000 pounds). The canyon route got a bit of a facelift in 1949 when the section between Yale and Lytton was widened and improved, but the southern route still allowed for the use of larger trucks and truck-trailer combinations. Most trucking companies sent their semi-trailer rigs bound for northern BC to Princeton, then via Merritt to Spences Bridge and on up the old Cariboo route. That situation prevailed until a new Alexandra Bridge opened in 1962, allowing longer, and heavier, rigs to use the Fraser Canyon as well.

Even with improvements to the main routes, there were remote areas of the province where truckers still experienced conditions reminiscent of the pioneer days. One of these was the Bridge River Valley in the Coast Mountains about 160 kilometres (100 miles) north of Vancouver. During

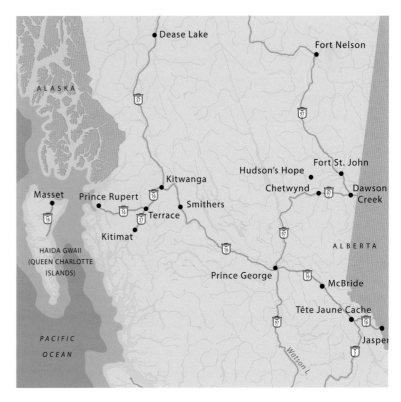

Above: Three drivers for Neal Evans Transportation pose in front of the company's small fleet of Hayes-Anderson trucks at Shalalth in the mid-1930s. Neil Evans was a pioneer trucker in the Bridge River country.

Above right: A Neal Evans' Hayes-Anderson truck, photographed at Bralorne mine in 1935.

Right: Another Bridge River pioneer was Albert Wihksne, whose Auburn is shown here in 1935 stuck in the mud on the Bridge River road. One of Neal Evans's Hayes-Andersons is waiting patiently in the background.

All photos courtesy of John Wihksne

the 1930s the Pioneer and Bralorne mines in the upper reaches of the valley were two of the most productive gold mines in the country, but it was postwar hydroelectric development that provided enhanced opportunities for the trucking industry. Between 1946 and 1960 BC Electric built three dams and four generating stations along with penstocks and tunnels to divert water from the Bridge River under Mission Mountain to the Seton Lake reservoir. This was the largest hydro development in the province until the huge dams built on the Peace and Columbia rivers in the 1960s. There was no direct road connection between the Fraser River at Lillooet and the Bridge River country. Trucks carrying equipment and supplies had to be loaded onto Pacific Great Eastern Railway flatcars and off-loaded at Shalalth, from where they drove up over Mission Mountain across a road made treacherous by switchbacks, rock slides and steep grades to connect with a road that followed the Bridge River west into the valley. "If there was a tougher piece of country to carry freight over, I never found it," wrote Andy Craig, who hauled into the Bridge River Valley in the mid-1930s.

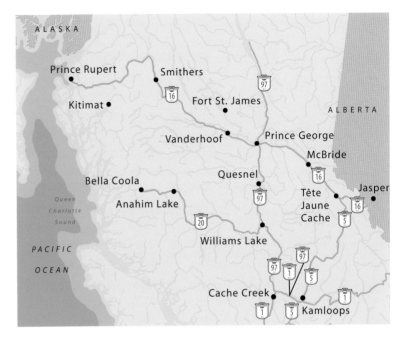

The route was inaugurated by Neal "Curly" Evans, a one-time wagon-train driver for the BX Line, who switched to trucks and in the 1920s began offering stage and freight service into the mining camps on the remote tributaries of the Bridge River. He was joined in 1934 by Red Doffner, who built up a fleet of fourteen trucks running between the mines and the railhead. In the mid-1930s, Evans began an all-season passenger bus service between Vancouver and the Pioneer mine as well. "A picturesque, almost legendary figure" was how *Motor Carrier* magazine described him, for his feats of trucking heavy equipment "through country that would break the heart of a mountain goat." Evans died in 1946.

In 1945 Albert Wihksne, a logging truck driver living in Gold Bridge, decided to challenge Evans for

A line of provincial public works department trucks wait to load up with gravel near Williams Lake in the 1920s. The gravel would be used to surface the Chilcotin Road.

Quesnel & District Museum and Archives, P2003.2.358.1

The Longest Worst Road

"During the 1960s and 1970s, Highway 20 may not have been the worst road in Canada, it may not even have been the worst road in the province, but its reputation as the longest worst road anywhere was never challenged."
— Diana French, Chilcotin Highway historian

Below: The Freedom Road was the steep stretch of Highway 20 from Anahim Lake west into the Bella Coola Valley. The residents had to build it themselves and the job was completed in July 1953 when two bulldozers from opposite directions touched blades. The road officially opened in July 1955.

Right: A traveller pauses at one of the switchbacks on the Big Hill to admire the view.

BC Central Coast Archives, Cliff Kopas Collection

a share of the local freight business by hauling occasional loads down to Vancouver. Evans complained to the Public Utilities Commission, the body that regulated provincial truck licensing, but the PUC gave Wihksne his general freight licence and in 1947 he began a scheduled service, Bridge River Vancouver Transport, running from the Bridge River Valley to the coast using a pair of Fargo trucks. Only eighty kilometres (fifty miles) of the trip was on pavement; the rest was on narrow gravel roads across mountain passes and along the sides of precipitous canyons. The worst section was Mission Mountain. "During the winter the south slope would be covered with snow slides," recalled John Wihksne, Albert's son; "any brief thaw followed by freezing temperatures would turn the road into a sheet of ice. During the summer, most vehicles would overheat before reaching the summit."

Albert Wihksne almost lost his life on one of these runs in January 1949. He and another driver, Edward Smith, were hauling a load of beer from Vancouver to supply the beer parlours in Bralorne and Gold Bridge. They were making their way along the fifty-five-kilometre (thirty-four-mile) stretch between Lytton and Lillooet, Wihksne in the passenger seat, when Smith hit a patch of ice and the truck slid off the road into the canyon. The vehicle came to rest against a tree stump about a third of the way down the slope. Wihksne was trapped under the truck and Smith walked twenty kilometres (twelve miles) to find help. John Wihksne believes his father never really recovered from the several hours he spent in the freezing cold waiting to be rescued; he died four and a half years later.

Another remote highway was the Chilcotin Road, a narrow, rutted strip of gravel and potholes winding westward from Williams Lake across the Chilcotin Plateau toward the Pacific. The road suffered from constant neglect. ("Why don't we just put a gate across it and a sign saying enter at your own risk?" one road foreman reportedly asked.) The province could not be convinced there were enough people on the plateau to warrant the expense of upgrading it. The first truck line servicing the scattered settlements belonged to Tommy Hodgson, a transplanted Yorkshireman who drove stage on the Cariboo

Road before taking over the Chilcotin mail run in 1912. Hodgson began using motor vehicles spring to fall and sleighs in the winter. He manufactured his first truck himself, taking a seven-passenger 1914 Cadillac touring car and replacing the back end with a truck box. When Hodgson died in 1945 his sons carried on their father's company as Hodgson Brothers. (It became Elliott Transport when they finally sold in 1961.)

The Hodgsons were joined in the 1930s by another freight carrier, Stan Dowling. Dowling initially came to the Chilcotin to visit his brother and stayed on to try his hand at raising cattle inland from Bella Coola. At that time settlers in the western Chilcotin had to have their supplies shipped by boat to Bella Coola, then carried up the mountain trails by pack train. Dowling decided it made more sense to truck supplies from the other direction. In 1934 he went down to Vancouver and purchased a used Ford. The dealer gave him a reduced price on the vehicle so long as Dowling promised that if he made it home safely he would advertise that a Ford was the only truck capable of driving the length of the Chilcotin Road. Once he proved it was possible, Dowling began making a regular freight run from Vancouver to Anahim Lake, where he also ran a store and post office. He eventually sold his freight licence and mail contract to the Hodgsons.

Bella Coola continued to be supplied by boat but residents wanted a road out of their valley up to Anahim Lake—and when the government refused to build it, they decided to do it themselves. Using a pair of bulldozers working from opposite ends, a crew pushed through seventy-six kilometres (forty-seven miles) of rock and forest. The new Social Credit government took pity on the townspeople and sent them the money, but it was the locals who built the road, which officially opened in July 1955. Even though it was not much better than a goat track, BC had its third road outlet to the Pacific.

The government continued to neglect the Chilcotin Road (Highway 20) until Alex Fraser, a trucker himself, came to its rescue. Fraser, a one-time partner in Wood and Fraser Transport hauling freight between Prince George and Vancouver, was also a prominent Cariboo politician and served twenty years as mayor of Quesnel before winning a seat in the provincial legislature in 1969. With the election of Bill Bennett's Social Credit government in 1975, Fraser joined the cabinet as minister of highways and transportation, a job he held for the next twelve years. It was the first time that someone who had actually driven the roads behind the wheel of a big rig was in charge of the province's highways. During Fraser's time in office, paving of the Chilcotin Road began, along with much-needed upgrades and improvements, and before too long the trip from Williams Lake to Anahim Lake, a drive that formerly could take days, was reduced to just four hours. Still, the Chilcotin route remains one of the most dangerous stretches in Canada to drive. The big hill down into the valley of the Bella Coola River is a switchback gravel road, sometimes narrowing to a single lane, with a gradient at times of eighteen percent, which makes it three times as steep as the Trans-Canada Highway through Rogers Pass.

Alex Fraser, minister of transportation and highways, makes an announcement related to the Coquihalla project in 1984. Fraser's career in the trucking industry dated back to the 1930s when he drove for Wood and Fraser Transport based out of Quesnel and Prince George. He was the only trucker ever put in charge of the province's roads and he took advantage of the situation to push ahead a variety of highway improvements.
Royal BC Museum, BC Archives I-68028

The post–World War II era ushered in an intense period of highway building in the province. It began while John Hart was still premier, and the first large project to be completed was named for him. The Hart Highway, which opened in 1952, connected Prince George to the Alaska Highway at Dawson Creek and opened the northern half of the province to trucks for the first time. The Hart opened just a few days after the election of W.A.C. Bennett and his Social Credit government, and it was the Socreds who oversaw the flurry of road building that characterized the next two decades.

The expansion of the road network depended on postwar developments in road-building technology, particularly in techniques for hard surfacing. The department of highways constructed its own

Above: A crowd of dignitaries watches cement being poured at the beginning of construction of the George Massey Tunnel under the Fraser River south of Vancouver in 1957.

Right: Another highway project built during the Socred era was the Port Mann Bridge, completed in 1964.

Royal BC Museum, BC Archives I-32378; Jewish Museum and Archives of BC, LF.02057, Otto Landauer photo

Highways minister Phil Gaglardi inspects the construction of the Terrace–Kitimat Highway at Hirsch Creek in 1956. Kitimat Museum & Archives, Northern Sentinel Collection 2005.8.695

asphalt plants and adopted new spreading machines and techniques that greatly increased the speed and efficiency of hard-surface road construction. But it was Bennett and his highways minister, Phil Gaglardi, who recognized that dependable roads were a key to vitalizing the economy of the Interior. Under their supervision, the share of the provincial budget devoted to highways doubled from ten percent to twenty percent, second only to spending on education, and several major projects were completed. These included the 1962 completion of the Vancouver–Blaine Freeway to the border, including the Massey Tunnel, which opened three years earlier; the opening of the Port Mann Bridge and the Fraser Valley section of the Trans-Canada from Taylor Way in West Vancouver to Agassiz in 1964 (Gaglardi promised that a motorist could drive from Vancouver to Chilliwack on the new Highway 1 in just forty-five minutes); and improvements to sections of Highway 3, the southern trans-provincial route. When the Socreds came to power, gravel highways still predominated throughout the Interior. By the end of the 1960s, asphalt surfaces were the norm as thousands of kilometres of highway were constructed or upgraded.

Not to be overlooked was the new attention paid to snow removal. Prior to the war very few mountain passes were kept open; as a result, trucking was very much reduced in the Interior during the winter. By the mid-1950s, however, the department of highways was keeping twice as many kilometres of roadway open during the winter than it had a decade earlier. This meant that the trucking industry could begin offering reliable year-round service more widely across the province.

Above: At Kootenay Pass in the Selkirk Mountains one-way traffic moves through an opening in the snow brought down onto the highway by a controlled avalanche. Once traffic is cleared, the rest of the snow is removed.

Left: In Rogers Pass the large mounds, known as avalanche traps, are intended to break up the avalanche flow so as to protect the highway.

Avalanche Control

It is not unusual during the winter in the interior of the province for a highway to be closed because of an avalanche, or the fear of an avalanche. The provincial ministry of transportation maintains a watch on sixty-two locations around the province that have been identified as avalanche prone. When they determine by weather and snowpack observations that an avalanche is likely to rumble across a highway, technicians will initiate a temporary road closure as a precaution. When conditions allow it, the technicians will cause an avalanche by dropping explosives from the air or by triggering remote control devices installed on the mountainside. In Rogers Pass, where the Trans-Canada Highway has the highest avalanche rating of any highway in North America, members of the Canadian Armed Forces clear the risk by firing howitzer shells high into the avalanche paths to bring down the snow.

It Made Life a Whole Lot Easier

"When I went to Cranbrook [in 1962 with CP Transport] the way for the trucks to get from Vancouver to Cranbrook was to drive up over the Hope Princeton to Osoyoos, then go down into the States, across Washington State to Kingsgate and then back up into Cranbrook. And of course the bureaucracy of what we had to do in those days because of the border was really something. It was in 1962 when the Blueberry Paulson Summit between Grand Forks and Castlegar opened that we could stop going through the States and of course it made life a whole lot easier."
— George Lloyd

Left: Makeshift bridges in the backcountry were always at risk of being washed away. Here a truck lies upside down in the Canoe River after a bridge collapsed. Valemount Historic Society, Valemount and Area Museum, No. 2003.10.8

Above: This early vehicle, on its way to Dease Lake on the Stewart–Cassiar Highway c. 1920s, has been adapted to carry both passengers and freight. Royal BC Museum, BC Archives E-01090

Left: A carefully loaded flat deck delivers a custom-cut over-length pole through the streets of Vancouver in 1942 accompanied by police escort. City of Vancouver Archives CVA 586-868, Don Coltman/Steffens Colmer photo

Opposite: A McGavin's bread van passes Vancouver City Hall in 1946. The company slogan was "Don't say bread, say McGavin's" and its trucks were a familiar sight around the province. City of Vancouver Archives CVA 586-4759, Don Coltman/Steffens Colmer photo

We Have to Create Transportation

"Luckily the people of British Columbia realized that if we're going to open our north country up we have to create transportation, and rail wasn't going to be the only answer. And it wasn't. It's proven nowadays that rail can't get the product in the same time frame as a truck can."
— *Frank Linke, trailer mechanic*

The extension of BC's road network had an impact on every aspect of life in the province. Communities that were formerly distant and isolated from each other were now accessible. Goods and services that were once confined to the major metropolitan areas could be delivered via the highways to all corners of the province. It is not an exaggeration to say that roads made a province-wide economy possible.

One of the businesses that took advantage of the road network to expand its operations from the Lower Mainland to the rest of the province was Woodward's, the iconic retail chain founded in 1902 by Vancouver merchant Charles Woodward. Woodward's had not had any trouble filling mail orders from customers who lived in the logging camps and stump farms of the coast; it simply loaded the groceries, hardware or dry goods aboard one of the Union Steamship vessels that plied a regular run between Vancouver and Prince Rupert and stopped every place in between. But delivering goods across Vancouver Island or into the Interior was more of a challenge, at least until the roads went in.

Woodward's opened its first store outside the Lower Mainland in Port Alberni in 1948 and with that, an era of expansion began. It was no accident their growth coincided with the opening of the Hope–Princeton Highway and then the upgrades to the Fraser Canyon road. Woodward's branches appeared in Victoria, Kamloops, Prince George, Abbotsford, Penticton and elsewhere. The growing chain used its own fleet of large-capacity trucks to service its stores along the new ribbons of blacktop. By the time

Top: Ferries are part of the highway system in BC. During the 1950s the Black Ball Line operated ferries on the south coast, providing a vital supply line to Vancouver Island. Here a pair of Merchant Cartage flatbeds await loading on the MV Kahloke in the mid-1950s.

Left: Today the BC Ferry Corp. operates one of the world's largest ferry systems and enables freight service to communities up and down the coast.

Courtesy of Dietmar Krause; David Nunuk photo

Opposite: A dump truck drives off one of the reaction ferries across the Fraser River, 1946. Reaction ferries run on cables and are propelled by the power of the river current.

The Exploration Place, Wally West Collection

Below opposite: Winter on the Coquihalla tests the driving skills of even the most experienced driver. Snow and icy conditions often close this stretch of highway. David Nunuk photo

Woodward's went out of business in the 1990s, the chain consisted of twenty-six department stores and thirty-three discount stores, all supplied by trucks running from the company's central warehouses in Vancouver. And the success of Woodward's was just one example of how the expansion of roads and trucking brought the benefits of the new consumer economy to all British Columbians, not just those who happened to live in the Lower Mainland.

Truck operators were happy to see the opening of the Trans-Canada Highway through Rogers Pass in 1962. These dignitaries are attending the first, unofficial opening staged by Premier W.A.C. Bennett at Revelstoke in July, a few weeks before Prime Minister John Diefenbaker made the official opening in the pass.

Courtesy of Dietmar Krause

One highlight of the Socred era was the completion of the Trans-Canada Highway across Rogers Pass. Finishing the national highway was a jointly funded project with costs shared by the federal government and the provinces and was initiated by the Trans-Canada Highway agreement in 1949. Work progressed more slowly than anticipated and in 1956, when the agreement expired, less than half of the new route was ready. The agreement was renewed with new financing arrangements and finally the last link in the national chain was closed with the completion of the road through Rogers Pass. The new route replaced the long-despised Big Bend Highway and cut hours off the drive for truckers. Prime Minister John Diefenbaker came out from Ottawa to officiate at the opening in Rogers Pass on September 3, 1962. Dignitaries from all the provinces attended but the host premier, W.A.C. Bennett, decided to boycott the event, sending Phil Gaglardi instead. In fact, Bennett tried to upstage Diefenbaker by

holding his own ribbon-cutting ceremony a month earlier, down the road in Revelstoke. Bennett was angry with Ottawa over the cost-sharing agreement and refused to share the stage with his federal counterpart. To further irritate the feds, Bennett later removed all the Trans-Canada Highway signs in BC and had them replaced with signs that read, simply, "British Columbia #1." No mention of Canada. When the New Democratic Party came to power in the 1972 election, the new government promptly reposted the Trans-Canada signs and BC rejoined Confederation.

By the 1970s British Columbia's modern road network was in place. Quality roads stretched north to the Peace River, west from Prince George to Prince Rupert, the length of Vancouver Island, over the interior mountain ranges and across the bottom of the province. With the major routes completed, government investment in new roads began to decline. This did not mean that highway megaprojects were a thing of the past, however, only that the emphasis shifted from construction to maintenance. There were still large projects to come, too, notably during the 1980s when the Socreds built the Coquihalla Highway connecting Hope via Merritt to Kamloops. (The work was completed amid much controversy; the cost of construction turned out to be two-thirds higher than the government had predicted and an inquiry revealed serious deficiencies in the administration of the undertaking.) In 1990 the Coquihalla Connector opened between Merritt and Kelowna, dramatically cutting travel times from the Lower Mainland to the central Okanagan. Harking back to the pre-war Fraser Canyon Highway, the Coquihalla was a toll road until 2008. But the Coquihalla—and the Island Highway upgrades of the 1990s—were the exception rather than the rule. Highway construction on a grand scale had become

Princess Margaret, the Queen's sister, cuts the ribbon to open the bridge across Okanagan Lake at Kelowna in July 1958.

Kelowna Public Archives

less politically acceptable and at the same time less necessary: by the end of the century all parts of the province enjoyed decent all-weather road connections. Today BC has 71,000 kilometres (44,000 miles) of two-lane roadways, sixty-eight percent of which are paved.

In the Lower Mainland, however, the challenge of traffic congestion became ever more pressing as the new millennium began. Transport Canada calculates the cost of lost productivity due to congestion at $1.5 billion a year. As well, slower traffic means increased smog and greenhouse gas emissions. The trucking industry lobbied persistently for improvements to the road system, arguing that the efficient movement of goods was crucial not just to local air quality but to the provincial and even the national economy. With the federal and provincial governments' increased emphasis on BC as Canada's "gateway" to the Asia-Pacific, it became evident that the pressure on local transportation infrastructure was only going to get worse. One critical choke point was the Port Mann Bridge, where traffic had increased by seventy percent since the mid-1980s. Studies showed that during daylight hours the bridge was congested ninety percent of the time.

Early in 2006 the provincial government officially unveiled its solution to the problem, announcing a $3 billion Gateway Program. Key components of the program include the twinning of the Port Mann Bridge, the widening of the Trans-Canada Highway into Vancouver and the construction of perimeter roads along the Fraser River. But the Port Mann and related projects form just one part of a much larger program aimed at addressing the challenges that face the transportation sector as it contemplates the anticipated expansion of trade with the Asia-Pacific.

Opposite: Construction work continues on the new Port Mann bridge in the summer of 2011. The twinning of the bridge is part of the $3 billion Gateway Program to improve traffic flow around Greater Vancouver.
Nick Procaylo/PNG

The Alex Fraser Bridge, shown here at night, crosses the Fraser River at New Westminster and is named for the former trucker and minister of transportation and highways.
David Nunuk photo

Horses to Horsepower

In 1898 the Robert Simpson Company, the pioneer Toronto department store, purchased the first motorized freight vehicle in Canada, a battery-powered delivery truck manufactured in Chicago by Fischer Equipment. Able to carry just ninety kilograms (two hundred pounds) of freight and with a top speed of twenty-two kilometres (fourteen miles) an hour and a range of sixty-five kilometres (forty miles) on a charge, this vehicle was more a novelty than an innovation—but it was a sign of things to come. The following year Parker's Dye Works, another Toronto company, acquired a Canadian-made electric delivery van and before long added a second, a Winton, manufactured by

Many of the earliest motor vehicles were powered by steam engines, like this wagon owned by John Duncan in the 1890s, looking like a cross between a truck and railway engine. But steam turned out to be a cumbersome technology and eventually the internal combustion engine prevailed. Royal BC Museum, BC Archives D-09370

the Canadian Cycle and Motor Company. At that point there were almost no paved roads beyond the city limits and few trucks offered service to the suburbs, but the appearance of the small urban delivery van marks the beginning of motorized trucking in Canada.

Above: P. Burns and Co. was a pioneer in the use of motorized delivery vans. This one was wheeling around Vancouver streets in 1926.

Bottom: James Stark, shown here beside his Oldsmobile in 1906, is credited with being the first person to operate a motorized truck in the city.

Royal BC Museum, BC Archives C-02401; City of Vancouver Archives, Trans P54

It did not take long for one of the newfangled motor vehicles to arrive in British Columbia. James Stark, owner of a dry goods store on Cordova Street in Vancouver and a founding member of the local automobile club, operated the first motorized delivery van in the city in about 1907. Before long larger businesses of all kinds were following Stark's lead. For example, P. Burns and Company, a large meat packer that also had a chain of retail meat outlets, was running a fleet of five delivery vans by 1912. The civic government was quick to innovate as well; in 1907 the city purchased three motorized trucks for its fire department, and Vancouver was the first city in Canada to have motorized firefighting equipment. Two years later the city also acquired a gasoline-powered ambulance; ironically, on its trial run it ran over an American tourist on Granville Street and killed him. William Mellis, a stage driver, pioneered distance trucking at about this time when he began a delivery service between Vancouver and

The Mellis chain-driven Gramm is shown here ascending the Granville Street hill at 15th Avenue on its way south toward Eburne in 1912. It was the first motor truck to venture out of the city along Granville Street and everyone along the route came out to see the horseless carriage pass by. *City of Vancouver Archives, Trans P89*

Eburne (Marpole), then a distant suburb on the north bank of the Fraser, with a chain-driven Gramm, a vehicle imported from Ohio. By 1912 the editors of the *Vancouver Sun* newspaper were complaining that the city's 1,769 motor vehicles were overcrowding local streets.

Meanwhile, in the Interior, the famed BC Express Company was making the transition to motorized freight. During the first decade of the twentieth century, the BX Line was still using horse and wagon. Freight came by rail to Ashcroft, then was off-loaded to wagons for the haul north up the old Cariboo Road. According to an article in the *Ashcroft News*, an average of 45,000 kilograms (100,000 pounds) a week was hauled to the various stops along the road by about a hundred wagons and dozens of pack trains. In total, there were in the neighbourhood of a thousand horses, oxen, mules and donkeys at work on the road at any one time, not to mention the BX stagecoach, which took four days to travel from Ashcroft to Barkerville. Blacksmith shops were the service stations of the day, shoeing horses and repairing ironwork on the wagons.

In 1910, in order to meet the looming threat of motorized competition, BC Express purchased a pair of Winton six-cylinder automobiles in Seattle and set them to work carrying passengers between Ashcroft and the steamer landing at Soda Creek. The Wintons, of which there were eight by 1913, operated in the summer months; during the winter they were refurbished at the express company's garage in Ashcroft while sleighs took over the job of hauling passengers. By the outbreak of World War I, all the horse-drawn freight wagons on the road had been replaced by trucks. And it was the same farther east. In Kamloops, for example, the first delivery truck arrived in 1910. Purchased by Dalgleish and Sons, a hardware and plumbing business, it was a McLaughlin from Oshawa, Ontario, with a two-cylinder

The Winton Six motor cars used on the Cariboo Road by the BC Express Company are shown here lined up at the company garage in Ashcroft in the 1920s. These vehicles carried passengers and baggage and were eventually replaced by freight trucks. Royal BC Museum, BC Archives A-09854

Buick engine. (The earliest interprovincial freight run in Canada occurred in 1913 when a Federal truck from the Canadian Motor Company carried a load of mattresses and bedsprings from Winnipeg to Regina, a trip of 570 kilometres—350 miles—that took four days.)

World War I accelerated the production of motor vehicles of all types but especially trucks. Assembly-line production was applied to the military effort and trucks were used in a variety of war-related activities. Following the war, these vehicles made the transition to civilian life along with their drivers,

Below: A Renard Road Train hauls a pair of wagonloads of wool bales in Queensland, Australia, c. 1915. The same vehicle had a brief but unsuccessful tryout in BC. Museum Victoria

A Train on Wheels

An intriguing attempt at pioneering long-distance trucking was the Canadian Renard Road Transportation Company, formed by a group of Vancouver businessmen, including Mayor Charles Douglas, in 1910. It utilized the Renard Road Train, a tractor-like vehicle hauling several six-wheeled trailers, which had been developed by a French military engineer. But it was slow and cumbersome and was soon scrapped.

Right: During the 1920s, motor mania swept Canada. The motor car went from being a novelty to a necessity and along with it, the motorized delivery vehicle became a must-have for businesses of all kinds, including this Chinatown produce company in Vancouver. City of Vancouver Archives CVA 2009-005.553

Below: In Nanaimo, W. E. Rumming used this converted motor car for making deliveries from his bottling works. Those are crates of bottles in the back.

Royal BC Museum, BC Archives D-04209

Left: The Rumming's bottling plant in Nanaimo was in operation from 1897 to 1954.

Below: A fleet of trucks belonging to the Reynolds Cartage Co. waits outside the Pacific Great Eastern Railway freight office in Vancouver, 1926.

Royal BC Museum, BC Archives D-04208; City of Vancouver Archives PAN N189, W.J. Moore photo

Bottom: Little Giant was one of the various models of motor trucks manufactured during the World War I era. This is the company's Vancouver branch with a pair of vehicles parked outside. City of Vancouver Archives CVA A17914, Stuart Thomson photo

It's easy to see how early crew transporters got the nickname "crummy." This converted car at a logging operation near Sproat Lake on Vancouver Island had zero protection from the elements—or the bumps. Alberni Valley Museum

swelling the ranks of the commercial fleet and accelerating the transition from horse power to horsepower. "The automotive industry is just becoming a factor in the transportation of passengers and freight in this country," remarked the *Canada Yearbook* of 1926. "Railways have found that the handling of less-than-carload lots of freight is often an unprofitable business. It follows that commercial trucks are being used in greater numbers…"

Early trucks carried from one to three tons of freight and, with thirty- to fifty-horsepower engines, could reach a top speed of perhaps twenty kilometres (twelve miles) per hour. Transmissions required the driver to double clutch for every gear change. A variety of truck models were on the roads up to and into the 1920s but the favourite was a Model T (later a Model A) Ford converted into a one-ton truck with the addition of a box of some kind in place of the back seats. Even though Ford itself began manufacturing a one-ton truck in 1918—the Model TT sold for just under a thousand dollars and had a top speed of twenty-eight kilometres (seventeen miles) per hour—the converted version remained popular.

When he got into the hauling business in Vancouver in 1929, Andy Craig acquired one of these vehicles from his father. Initially it was a dump truck, which Craig used to haul gravel and dirt for the city. "It was hard work to operate," he recalled. "Other truck contractors for the city were supplying dual-tired, hydraulic-operated dump trucks, and we were still using strong-arm methods: getting out of the cab to undo the latch and putting our shoulders under the balance of the load to tip it, before driving away." Before long Craig added sideboards and a canvas top to the old Ford and began moving furniture from neighbourhood to neighbourhood.

As the road system improved so did the early vehicles. Pneumatic tires began to replace the hard rubber variety, taking some of the jarring bump and grind out of the ride. As maximum speeds increased, better braking systems had to be developed. Still, driving remained a challenge, especially in the Interior. On a regular run up the Fraser Canyon and across to Penticton during the Depression,

As motor vehicles came into wider use, garages opened to service them. This photograph shows a garage in Cloverdale, east of Vancouver, in the 1910s. The mechanic stands on the left beside his dog. The operation seems to be a popular place with the neighbourhood children, attracted by the chance to see one of the newfangled automobiles.

Royal BC Museum, BC Archives C-02709

a truck would bounce along for close to five hundred kilometres (three hundred miles) over deeply rutted washboard. Axles and springs could only withstand such a beating for a few months, at which point the front wheels were likely to drop off without warning. Even with improvements, trucks were underpowered and underbraked. Uphill speeds were less than fifteen kilometres (nine miles) an hour, and because brakes were unreliable, trucks crept downhill in low gear, the drivers afraid of losing control. Trips were measured in days, not hours; it could take four days to run from Vancouver to the Okanagan. There were no sleepers; drivers would put in at one of the truck stops along the way, pay a dollar for dinner and a room, then drive on the next day. Lumbering up long hills in the lowest gear in warm weather, it got so hot in the cab that drivers would lock the throttle in place and stand outside on the running board, steering through the window until the engine overheated and more water had to be added to the radiator. The Model B Ford was notorious for the faulty float valve in its carburetor. Going downhill the engine often backfired through the carburetor and set the front end on fire. Drivers knew to carry a pail of sand for just such an emergency.

Wine in the Ditch

"One rainy night after a particularly heavy cloudburst we found ourselves outside Cache Creek carrying seven tons of Calona Wine. Coming onto a bad stretch of muddy road, the truck just slipped into the quagmire until the box was level with the ground. We had no way of getting out until the department of highways trucks from Ashcroft would rescue us. They worked all the next morning, hauling gravel to make a new road, and finally got us out of the mess at three p.m."
— *Bert Wise, former driver*

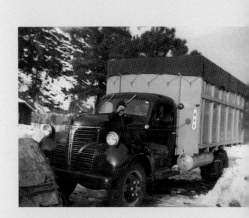

The All-Purpose Truck

"In those days [the 1930s] they were basically five-ton trucks but they hauled seven, eight tons and more sometimes to make it pay. And the trucks didn't have the driver-friendly technology of today. In those days they weren't specified for the job they did. You bought a truck and made whatever you wanted out of it: a gravel truck, a freight truck, whatever. They were pretty simple in technology. So there were no comforts, no air ride or anything. Most of the drivers had back problems after a very few years of pounding over the potholes in the road."
— *John Wihksne, former driver*

Above: This five-ton 1947 Fargo was one of two used by Albert Wihksne to establish Bridge River Vancouver Transport. Note the wooden freight box and the canvas tarpaulin to cover the cargo. That's Albert in the driver's seat with son John on the fender.
Courtesy of John Wihksne

Left: Carson Truck Lines, based in Quesnel, was one of the important carriers between Prince George and the coast. This 1963 photograph shows driver George Reddicop beside one of the straight trucks that replaced the pre-war, tarp-over models.
Courtesy of Bruce Harger

But to dwell on the limitations of the vehicles is to miss the important point that this was a period of rapid expansion and innovation. In 1932 the government issued just 162 public freight licences in the province; by 1937 that number had climbed to a thousand freight trucks and large vans, and the figure was rising steadily. With the introduction of tandem axles, the size of cargoes increased from an average of five tons to double that amount. The appearance of refrigerated vans ("reefers") during the 1930s meant that summer or winter fresh produce and frozen foods could be added to the long haul. Initially the cargo was cooled with ice or dry ice; in the 1950s the first compact refrigerating plants appeared, small enough to be built right into the trailers. The earliest units were attached to the bottom sides of the trailer but they were susceptible to damage by flying debris so they were moved to the front above the cab.

Going Radial

"I think the biggest change was radial tires. It was a really big improvement. I got a brand new International in 1971 and it had radial tires on it. A bias ply tire has a tube in it. They have a liner and if it went flat for some reason and you didn't notice it, that tube would start going around inside the tire, generate heat from friction and burst into flames. You had to stop quite often to check the tires. Radial tires were tubeless and didn't have this problem. They also gave a softer ride. You had to get used to them. They'd roll a little bit more

Refrigerated technology made great strides during the 1950s. This is one of the early "reefer" units. Courtesy of Dietmar Krause

on corners. But after you got used to them, they were great. That's another thing that's changed. Years ago we'd carry spares and have to change the tires ourselves. With radial tires you just went to the next tire shop, slowed down a bit maybe, but you didn't have to worry so much about heat."
— Bruce Shantz, former driver

By the mid-1950s there were three times as many registered vehicles in the province as there had been at the onset of the war. Truck-trailer combinations appeared with the opening of the Hope–Princeton route in 1949, replacing straight trucks for the long haul because of their larger carrying capacity and also because of increased efficiency and versatility. Trailers could be picked up and dropped off at a depot for unloading by someone other than the driver, and a single tractor could pull a variety of different specialized trailers. The shorter Fraser Canyon route was still limited to straight trucks—just over twelve metres (forty feet) maximum length and 18,000 kilograms (40,000 pounds) weight. "If you were over 40,000 pounds the scale man at Flood would tell you you had to go around [via Princeton, Merritt and Spences Bridge]," recalled Bruce Harger, who drove the route in those days supplying Overwaitea stores in the Cariboo. And if the freight was over 30,500 kilograms (68,000 pounds) it had to travel via Kamloops because the vehicles were too heavy for the bridges on the Merritt–Spences Bridge section.

In 1962 improvements to the Alexandra Bridge bottleneck made the use of larger rigs possible in the Fraser Canyon. These included the truck and pup, a straight truck with a trailer attached, and the train, a tractor towing usually two trailers, sometimes three. In 1963 Carson Truck Lines inaugurated the first double-trailer service via the canyon. Using a Kenworth tractor powered by a 280-horsepower

The truck and pup was a configuration that gained popularity during the 1960s. It consisted of a straight truck with a trailer attached and provided the carrier with more flexibility. In this case the truck was a Hayes cab-over and trailer, followed by an International tractor trailer, both hauling for Chapmans Freight Lines. Courtesy Bruce Shantz

Public Freightways ran this dual-trailer rig between Cranbrook and Vancouver. It featured a four-wheel drive tractor, which was expected to help over the mountain passes, but for a variety of reasons it didn't work out and the experiment ended after a couple of years. Note the chains hanging from the sides of the rig. Courtesy of Dietmar Krause

Rempel was the tanker division of Johnston Terminals, one of the giants of the industry. This 1973 combination features a tank on the tractor and then a 35-foot pup trailer attached with a draw hitch. Drivers referred to it as the tail wagging the dog. Courtesy of Dietmar Krause

Cummins diesel, Carson hauled two seven-metre (twenty-four-foot) trailers from Vancouver to Williams Lake, where one of the trailers was dropped off. Another tractor picked up the second trailer for delivery to Quesnel while the original tractor returned to the coast hauling two new trailers. The overall length of this setup was twenty metres (sixty-five feet). Doubles, with their increased freight capacity, soon became the industry standard for long-distance hauling everywhere in the province. Few innovations have been as significant in the history of long-haul freighting as the transition from straight trucks to tractor-trailer combinations.

Air brakes, lightweight aluminum trailers, CB radios, these were just some of the other innovations that appeared in the postwar era. Bert Wise reported that in 1937 he began driving a Leyland diesel with tandem axles and a metal box for Fred Hunt, a Langley-based operator, but diesels were rare in the pre-war years. They really came into their own in the 1950s, six-cylinders to begin with, then V8s in the following decade. That opened the way for the Jake brake, an engine compression brake that came into use as a safety feature on the diesels in the 1960s. The brake works by restricting the release

There was more to driving a truck than sitting behind the wheel. In the early days the job description involved lots of heavy lifting. Here a driver loads sacks of flour into the delivery van at the Ogilvie Flour Mills on Homer Street in Vancouver in 1935. City of Vancouver Archives CVA 99-4824, Stuart Thomson photo

Here a couple of men are shifting bags of coal from a Kirk Company truck on Main Street in Vancouver in 1932. Kirk began business in 1897 delivering coal and ice, later branching out into home heating systems. City of Vancouver Archives CVA A18223, Stuart Thomson photo

of compressed air from the engine cylinders, slowing the vehicle. The idea was the driver didn't have to ride the brake pedal coming down inclines, saving the brakes from getting hot. Because of BC's steep terrain, drivers here adopted Jake brakes more widely than in other jurisdictions. They were unpopular with the public because they were so noisy and their use is still restricted in many built-up areas, but more recent models have gone a long way toward muffling the sound. Today's long-haul drivers will employ their engine brakes much more frequently on a trip than their wheel brakes.

Mechanized loading and unloading, especially through the use of forklifts, relieved drivers and dock workers of much of the manual labour that had been part of the job since the beginning, yet it arrived slowly. When John Bourbonniere began his career shifting freight around the loading dock in the mid-1960s, he recalled, almost none of it was palletized. It was "fingerprint" freight; that is, someone had to manually lift it on and off the truck (a job known as "handbombing"). By the end of the decade, most shippers had been convinced to put their freight on pallets and forklifts were doing the bulk of the loading.

Above: The arrival of the forklift made the job a lot easier, as did the palletization of freight. Here cartons of Sun-Rype apple sauce are being loaded into a Chapmans trailer in Kelowna. Kelowna Public Archives, 4875

Right: A vehicle from the Johnston Terminals demolition division dumps waste using a snorkel, a hydraulic hoist devised by the company for lifting refuse containers.

Courtesy of Dietmar Krause

Keep Track of the Pallets

"Having managed one of Canada's largest warehousing and distribution companies, I can assure you the greatest problem with the introduction of pallets (otherwise a remarkable advantage for all) was pallet inventory control. Pallets got lost, damaged, stolen. Customers who surrendered their pallets to truckers naturally expected them returned—and in good condition, not a pile of firewood. We often saw our pallets, prominently marked with a red logo JTL, in other operators' warehouses or vans or dumped in back alleys or behind buildings. Pallet inventory controls were absolutely imperative, and a very time-consuming, frustrating and costly job."

— *Harvie Malcolm, Johnston Terminals*

Early drivers were captains of their own ships; they had no communication with their warehouses beyond the odd telephone call and employers had no means of monitoring their fleet or their drivers. This situation changed in the 1950s with the introduction of the tachograph. This instrument was attached to the vehicle and recorded a variety of measurements, including truck speed, time of day, gear use and so on, on a circular chart. When analyzed, the chart could be used to evaluate the performance of both the vehicle and the driver. Subsequently the tachograph was replaced by computers and GPS systems that collect an even more complete record of vehicle use and driver performance. Truck location can now be monitored by satellite tracking and the vehicle located to within a few metres. Customers can use the internet to track their own shipments. The latest innovation is the electronic on-board recorder, also known as a "black box," an electronic device attached to the vehicle that monitors a driver's hours of service, replacing paper log books.

The cab of a modern truck, like this Kenworth model, resembles the flight deck of an airplane. No one says the job of a driver is easy, but compared to fifty years ago the ride is smooth and there is no more wrestling through the changes with a pair of gear shifts.

David Nunuk photos

Trucks and railways have been constant competitors in the freight business but they have also cooperated in important ways. Here a load of short poles from a mill are stacked into a rail car in Quesnel in 1945.

Royal BC Museum, BC Archives I-27163

At the same time, containerization was revolutionizing the freight business. An early form of containerization involved the railways in a system known as piggyback; i.e., putting trailers directly onto rail flatcars to be carried across the country. Piggyback started between Montreal and Toronto in 1952 and then expanded across the country. In part it was an attempt by the railways to win back business they had lost during the 1950 national rail strike. So popular was the service that in 1968 the *Victoria Daily Colonist* newspaper ran an article predicting the end of long-haul trucking since it would surely be replaced by the piggyback service. The article argued that piggyback reduced labour costs for freight companies and improved highway safety by getting the big rigs off the road. The railways "are winning back a lot of the lucrative business they lost 10 to 15 years ago when the big road trailers were winning popularity [as a result of the nationwide rail strike]," the *Colonist* told its readers. (Within the province, the PGE, later BC Rail, operated a piggyback service from the Lower Mainland to Prince George and the north. It continued from the 1960s until 2002, despite complaints from the trucking industry that a publicly owned and therefore subsidized railway should not be competing with private sector carriers.)

Another advantage to rail not mentioned by the *Colonist* was that shippers were not constrained by the weight regulations of road travel. They paid a flat rate for a trailer going by rail, but they could put an extra amount of weight into it; in other words, they were earning extra revenue for no extra cost of operation. However, the railway companies eventually began to be concerned about the weight of the trailers and the wear and tear they were causing on the rail infrastructure. They put a stop to overweight loads, bringing an end to one of the cost advantages of shipping by rail. In addition, by the 1970s, the

service factor had become more important. Customers were moving toward just-in-time inventory management. Instead of having goods sitting in a warehouse, they wanted them delivered as they were needed. As a result, carriers no longer wanted to farm out the line haul to rail, with the possibility of delays over which they had no control. For a variety of reasons, then, rail piggyback service became a less attractive option for long-haul shipping.

Of course the use of containers to ship goods long distances has continued to expand. Hauling containers to and from the ports is a specialized form of trucking that involves dedicated equipment and licensing. This branch of the industry is highly fragmented, with about two hundred companies authorized to serve the Port Metro Vancouver docks, amounting to more than two thousand trucks. In 2010 more than 2.5 million containers arrived or departed through Port Metro Vancouver; about fifty percent of them were transported by truck, the rest by rail. For the truckers, many of whom are owner-operators, the work consists primarily of hauling containers filled with Asian-made consumer goods from the on-dock terminals to warehouses and distribution centres for transhipment, hauling containers loaded with exports to the terminals for overseas shipping and repositioning empty containers. Since 2007 the Port of Prince Rupert has also had an intermodal container shipping terminal in operation, though most of its containers move by rail.

Goods from overseas are loaded onto trucks at Port Metro Vancouver's Centerm container terminal. In 2010 more than 2.5 million containers moved through the port, fifty percent of them on a truck. Courtesy of Port Metro Vancouver

Following pages: A steady stream of container trucks flows away from Deltaport, Port Metro Vancouver's largest container terminal, located at Roberts Bank. David Nunuk photo

For many years the Hayes company was located in this building on West
Second Avenue in an industrial section of Vancouver. Hayes was known for its
heavy-duty off-highway vehicles but it made trucks of all types; for instance,
this Hayes-Anderson water wagon manufactured for the city, c. 1933.

City of Vancouver Archives, CVA 99-4290, Stuart Thomson photo

British Columbia has never been a major truck manufacturing centre but there have been notable exceptions, the most successful being the story of Hayes Trucks. In 1920 Douglas Hayes, owner of a parts company, and W.E. Anderson, a Quadra Island entrepreneur, set up shop in Vancouver as the Hayes-Anderson Motor Co. Ltd. to make trucks designed for the rough conditions of west coast lumber camps and other off-road heavy-duty jobs. For their first two years in business Hayes and Anderson were dealers for other manufacturers but in 1922 they began building their own model of logging truck. Six years later the company moved to a plant on Second Avenue, the industrial area that was home to many equipment manufacturers. At the same time Anderson withdrew from the operation, which changed its name to Hayes Manufacturing, though Hayes-Anderson remained the model name until 1934. Over the years the company expanded to build a variety of truck types—tankers, dump trucks, moving vans—plus buses. As well, Hayes became a distributor during the 1930s for British-made Leyland trucks. But it was heavy-duty logging trucks for which the company was best known. Its HDX series truck, which it began manufacturing in 1952, was one of the most popular logging trucks ever built.

In 1969 Mack Trucks bought a two-thirds interest in Hayes, and the company entered a period of expansion. At its peak, Hayes employed six hundred people at three Vancouver plants and was producing six hundred trucks a year with annual sales of about $20 million. One example of the kinds of challenges Hayes was asked to solve was that of a unique northern log-hauling operation that began in 1970. Logs were being moved from Ootsa Lake on the Nechako Plateau westward across the mountains to tidewater. A fifty-five-kilometre (thirty-four-mile) road was built across the summit of Sandifer Pass down to Kemano Bay where the logs were collected for towing to the Eurocan pulp mill at Kitimat. Hayes built twenty-six HDX 100-ton truck and trailer units to do the job. Every day during the open season, seven days a week, twenty hours a day, the big trucks hauled logs back and forth along this remote gravel road. The twenty-six trucks comprised the largest single order Hayes had ever received.

In 1974, Gearmatic Co., a subsidiary of Paccar Inc., a Seattle-area manufacturer, bought controlling interest in the company. The following year Paccar shut Hayes down and BC's largest truck manufacturer disappeared after fifty-five years. But the legacy lived on. Back in 1947 three former Hayes employees—Claude Thick, Vic Barclay and Mac Billingsley—had founded their own company to manufacture heavy-duty trucks and trailers, particularly for the logging industry. Pacific Truck and Trailer built vehicles for most of the big players in forestry, including MacMillan Bloedel and Crown Zellerbach, as well as for overseas customers. In 1970 International Harvester purchased the company, by this time

Top: Dave McIntosh hauls a big load of cedar with his Hayes HDX at Kwatna Bay in 1994.

Below: Pacific Truck and Trailer, another BC manufacturer, made this pair of heavy-duty vehicles, working the woods on Vancouver Island.

Courtesy of Dave McIntosh; courtesy of Bob Dingsdale

Top: This 1975 Pacific logging truck was rebuilt in 1984 when Alex Spenser (at end, right) became the driver. Spenser is joined in this photograph by (l. to r.) Ed Willis, Dwayne McKenzie, Bob Creighton and Barry Forbes.

Right: This 1974 Pacific P9 is owned by Chuck Carosella in Ladysmith.

Alberni Valley Museum; Kevin Oke photo

An insignia decorates the hood of a Kenworth.

David Nunuk photo

located in North Vancouver. IH continued to operate Pacific as a separate entity and continued to build vehicles for destinations in Asia, Africa and across North America. In 1981 IH was experiencing financial trouble and sold Pacific to a Singapore company and eventually, with the market for logging trucks shrinking, Pacific stopped producing; the factory closed in late 1991. The company continued as a supplier of heavy-duty parts and when a new owner consolidated its operations in Alberta in 2002, New Westminster–based Coast Powertrain Ltd. purchased the proprietary business—that is, Pacific's blueprints, moulds and templates dating back a half century—and continues to operate it as Pacific Truck Manufacturing Inc., repairing and servicing Pacific parts.

There were three other, more short-lived, BC-based manufacturing operations. One was Canadian Kenworth, a subsidiary of the American company, which opened a production facility in Burnaby in 1955. It made Kenworths for the Canadian market until 1982 when production shifted to Montreal. A second BC manufacturer was Freightliner of Canada. Founded during the 1940s in Portland, Oregon, Freightliner was one of the most successful makers of heavy-duty diesel trucks in North America, particularly known for its cab-over-engine models (COEs). In 1961 it decided to open a Canadian operation at a plant, also in Burnaby, where it produced vehicles until it was closed in 1991 during an economic downturn in the industry. By then Freightliner was owned by the German manufacturer Daimler-Benz. Interestingly, Daimler was also involved with the province's last major truck maker, Western Star. Started in Kelowna in 1967 by the White Motor Co., Western Star was a successful manufacturer of high-quality trucks for the military and resource industries overseas. It was purchased by Daimler's truck division (by then DaimlerChrysler), still based in Portland, in 2000 and the Kelowna facility was closed, marking the end of truck manufacturing in the province.

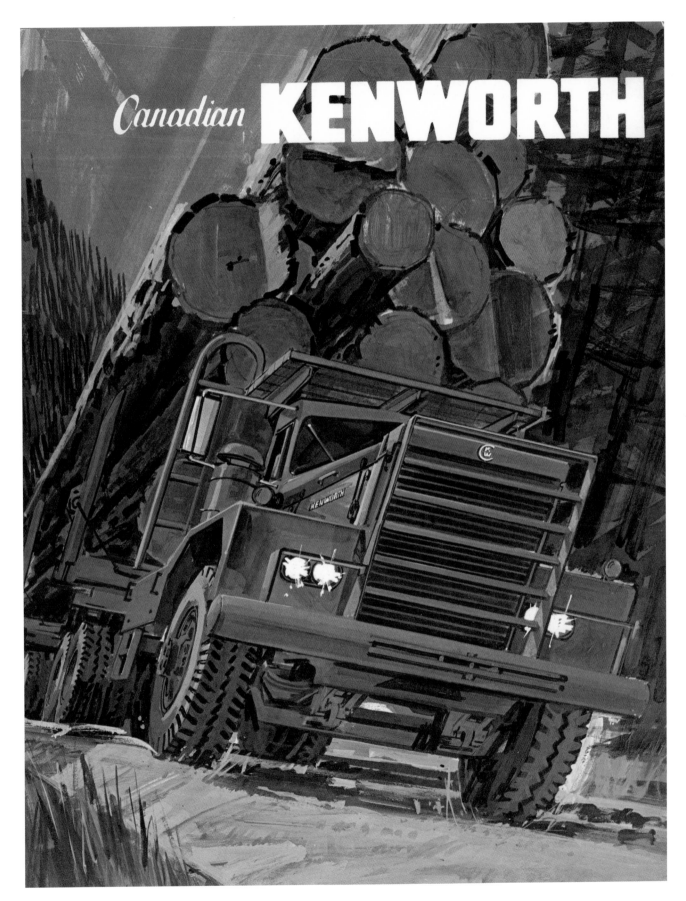

Canadian **KENWORTH**

Kenworth manufactured trucks at its Burnaby facility from 1955 to 1982 when production shifted to Montreal. This is one of the brochures from that period.

Courtesy of Bruce Shantz

The half-shack was an experiment in cab design that didn't last very long. They were also known as telephone booths or CBEs (cab beside engine).

Half-Shack on Fire

"My first job as an over-the-road driver was in 1956 with an outfit called Expressways, based in Vancouver. Expressways was started by Derek Wilkes when he returned from the war and it was an LTL outfit. Early on someone at Kenworth sold him four 'half-shacks.' These weren't just strange looking; they were the weirdest things on the road. The driver sat in a tiny compartment offset to the left side, similar to a crane truck. There were two seats but the buddy seat was located behind the driver, kind of like a fighter plane. There was a sleeper compartment crossways behind the engine.

"One evening in December of 1956 one of our lads was climbing Anarchist Mountain east of Osoyoos when his half-shack developed a coolant leak. He noticed the heat gauge rising so he pulled over to have a look. A local bread delivery driver in a two-ton Chevy stopped and between this pair of mechanical wizards they decided diesel fuel was almost the same as anti-freeze so they drained some of the fuel tanks and topped up the radiator. Diesel fuel and anti-freeze are not the same. Before he reached the top of the summit this so-called coolant boiled out onto the hot exhaust manifold, caught fire and the tractor burned to the ground. When the charred hulk was trucked back to the Kenworth plant in Burnaby someone decided it was an inherent problem of half-shacks so they rebuilt them into a conventional."
— *Ted Campbell, former driver*

Trucks have been essential in every part of the provincial economy but perhaps nowhere have they proven their worth more than in the forest industry. Whether hauling logs from the cut site to the dump site or the mill, lumber from the mill to the construction site, wood chips to the pulp mill, hog fuel or paper products, trucks have played a crucial role in every aspect of the forest sector since they began replacing railways in the woods.

A driver prepares to descend a timber road in the beginning days of truck logging, c. 1925. Note the hard rubber tires and complete lack of protection for the driver. Royal BC Museum, BC Archives F-08717

Trucks began venturing into the woods in significant numbers during the 1920s, when loggers realized that wheeled vehicles could reach stands of timber that rail could not, and at a lower cost. In terrain too steep for laying track, or where the timber was not plentiful enough to warrant a full-blown railway operation, trucks proved their worth, especially to small operators with limited resources. It took a daredevil of a driver to take the wheel of these early vehicles, with their hard tires and wonky brakes, and manhandle them across a slippery plank road or down a steep mountain path. Road-building equipment was in its infancy so for the most part the early trucks travelled on wood roads made of planks or logs, built on the model of small railway trestles. With the advent of bulldozers and crawler tractors, it became possible to build decent all-weather roads into the backcountry and along the sides of steep mountains.

A crew loads a logging truck bound for the Eagle Lake sawmill near Giscome in the 1940s. By this time the trucks had a few more comforts for the drivers but it was still a job for daredevils. Royal BC Museum, BC Archives F-09201

Frost on the Roads

"We used to get a hoar frost on the plank roads. You'd take one load over that and it would pack down, it was just like glass. But the superintendent was good. Most of the hills were rip-rapped with straw lines from the donkeys [steam engines] that were not used anymore, we used to use that for rip-rapping. And on the mornings when it was real bad, the superintendent would load the old crummy [an open cart] with sand and sand those hills. We never lost a load due to frost or anything."
— *Jake Wall, former driver*

Right: The rear wheels of this Duplex, skidding logs on a plank road in 1924, are wrapped with cable for additional traction. Museum at Campbell River 5134

Right: An advertising setup displays a late-model White truck and associated products in Prince George, 1948. Based in Cleveland, White began producing logging trucks in 1913 and was one of the few early manufacturers to survive beyond World War II. White trucks were among the most popular logging vehicles in BC for many years. The Exploration Place, Wally West Collection

Pacific built off-highway trucks specially designed for logging BC's rough terrain. This one has been adapted for skidding logs at East Fraser Logging, c. 1957. Courtesy of Bob Dingsdale

For the most part the early trucks didn't even have cabs, or windshields. Even doors were optional; sometimes it was better not to have any if you lost your brakes on a steep downhill run and had to bail out. Speaking of brakes, they tended to overheat and set the wheels on fire. Logging took a heavy toll on tires. Early pneumatic tires that might suit a highway hauler were of little use to a truck logger who needed a deep tread for the soggy ground and durable sidewalls to stand up to the heavy workout coming down the steep gravel roads. It was Goodyear that came out with a twelve-ply rayon cord tire during the Depression and set a new standard for pneumatic tires.

Some of the favourite truck models were Duplex, Gotfredson, Diamond T, White, Mack, Kenworth and of course the homegrown Hayes. By the 1930s dual-axle trailers capable of handling much heavier loads were gaining popularity. By this time, trucking contractors were taking on much of the work. These were people who were truckers first, loggers only secondarily. Logging companies contracted out to these contractors, whose job it was to move the logs from the cut.

Right: This experimental super-truck built by S. Madill of Nanaimo had a V16 engine and could haul 200-ton loads with trailer. Shown here at the Crofton Pulp and Paper Mill on Vancouver Island.

Below: Another big rig loaded with hemlock, cedar and Douglas fir makes its way across a causeway at a Sproat Lake logging operation, c. 1950.

Cowichan Valley Museum & Archives 1977.01.2.3; UBC Library, Rare Books and Special Collections, MacMillan Ltd. fonds, BC 1930/326

Say Again?

"It was exhausting work driving one of those trucks, and it only got harder when they moved off the planks and onto the dirt roads. Then the driver had to fight mud, rocks and ruts, all of which could grab the front wheels, tear the steering wheel out of his hands and aim his vehicle for the ditch. All the while the driver was sitting a couple of feet behind a screaming gas engine in an age of primitive muffler technology, and just above a gearbox that by itself made more noise than all the steam engines on the south coast combined. When you talk to old-time truckers you usually have to yell, or remind them to turn up their hearing aids."
— *Ken Drushka, logging historian*

These details are from a 1951 Mack A-40H owned by Tony Splane. Macks began appearing in the BC woods in the late 1930s and proved themselves a match for the rugged west coast conditions. Kevin Oke photos

This beautifully reconditioned 1956 International Harvester R200 is owned by Bill Robertson of Cowichan Lake. Kevin Oke photo

VINTAGE
7327
BRITISH COLUMBIA

The tough times of the Depression had the effect of reducing the number of logging truck manufacturers. Smaller makers went under and the post–World War II era was dominated by large manufacturers such as Mack, White, Kenworth and Hayes. By this time trucks had replaced almost all rail operations. The war had produced a surplus of military trucks and after the war the rugged vehicles flooded the market. Many logging operators purchased these leftover trucks and adapted them to working in the woods.

As the years passed, logging trucks got steadily larger and more powerful. In his master's degree thesis on trucking, Rhys Evans, a former driver, notes that while line haul operations have always been considered the industry standard, in fact it was off-highway logging equipment that pushed the limits of technology. "When 350 horsepower diesel highway tractors were the standard on the highway," Evans writes, "off-road logging trucks were operating with 600 horsepower Detroit Diesel engines coupled with Allison automatic transmissions, hauling loads of as much as forty tons."

Top: Operating on unregulated roads, production-hungry loggers strained the limits of conventional truck design.

Above: Timber giant MacMillan Bloedel opens its Cameron Lake division west of Port Alberni on Vancouver Island in 1965. The Hayes HDX, (front) and Pacific P16 (rear) were supersized off-highway trucks hand-built for the logging industry in BC.

Right: A Pacific in action on Vancouver Island.

Courtesy of Hank Rabe; UBC Library, Rare Books and Special Collections, MacMillan Bloedel fonds BC 1930/137/2; David Nunuk photo

In the late 1970s truck technology entered a period of rapid innovation, driven by a variety of factors. At about this time the provincial government agreed to an increase in the allowable gross vehicle weight, from 55,000 to 63,500 kilograms (120,000 pounds to 140,000 pounds), and at the same time introduced a minimum power-to-weight ratio in response to public complaints about getting stuck behind slow trucks on steep grades. This meant that vehicles required higher-powered engines to haul heavier weights and to maintain steady speeds on the highways. Horsepower in highway trucks began to climb from the 300 to 350 range that was the norm in the middle of the decade to the 425 horsepower that became the industry standard by the end of the 1980s. Today's tractor-trailer outfits running around the city may still have 350 to 400 horsepower, but the average truck out on the highway is now powered by a 475 to 500 horsepower engine. And when it comes to heavy haul, for example dump trucks or heavy equipment haulers, the vehicles average 525 to 550 horsepower, and sometimes higher. Similarly torque (the measure of an engine's ability to turn a shaft against a load and thus maintain speed on grades) increased from a maximum of perhaps 1,200 foot/pounds to the 1,800 foot/pounds that is fairly common in highway trucks today.

But vehicle weight and engine power were just part of the story. The 1970s also saw a growing concern about air quality and the first attempts to clean up engine exhaust emissions to conform to ever more stringent federal government requirements. The objective was to control the internal combustion process so that an engine coughed fewer emissions into the atmosphere. The first devices were throttle control mechanisms, which attempted to manage the fuel-to-air ratio so as to reduce the plumes of black smoke issuing from a vehicle's exhaust system. These mechanical controls were succeeded during the following decade by electronic controls that evaluate engine load and release only enough fuel

Engine technology has come a long way in the thirty years between the truck under construction in 1979 (above) and the modern engine of today (left) with its computer-driven electronic controls and advances in emission treatment.

Courtesy of Bob Dingsdale; David Nunuk photo

to meet the need. Interestingly, much of the product testing for electronics was done in BC because of the unique demands the province puts on vehicles. "If you want to break something, come to BC," explains Detroit Diesel's Mal Shephard. "We've got everything going against us. We've got very high loads, we've got grades, we've got varying operating conditions, from warm, humid conditions on the coast to brutally cold up in the Peace. And a truck can go through all that in a couple of days. So it's a great testing environment."

With electronic controls it became possible to reduce the nitrogen oxides (NOx) produced by the combustion process, which are the oxides that have the most significant impact on air quality. In addition, after-treatment devices were installed to clean the exhaust after it left the engine. Some of these advances came at a cost to drivers and owners in the form of mechanical problems and a negative impact on fuel economy. But in the end, the industry has succeeded in meeting the emissions standards set for it by the government. "With the trucks that are out there today, you can pretty well breathe the exhaust, it is coming out so clean," says Ray Cotton, the general manager for the truck dealer Inland Kenworth in Langley.

At the same time, the fuel itself has become much cleaner. By 2007 the sulphur content in diesel fuel had been reduced by ninety-seven percent, which was significantly cleaner than diesel fuel used in the marine and rail sectors. Along with ultra-low sulphur diesel fuel, now the industry standard, there is interest in alternative fuels, principally natural gas, either liquefied (LNG) or compressed (CNG). In 2011 Vedder Transport in Abbotsford became only the second trucking company in Canada to install

Vedder Transport, based in Abbotsford, specializes in the movement of liquid and dry bulk freight. The company is a pioneer in the use of liquefied natural gas to fuel its fleet of trucks. David Nunuk photo

The application of aerodynamic styling to truck design began back in the 1970s. This pair of tractors show how far manufacturers have come in adopting design features that decrease air resistance. David Nunuk photo

A lineup of late model trucks illustrates the slope nose, rounded bumpers and overall smooth design of the modern highway truck.
David Nunuk photo

Opposite: A modern rig hauling a pair of trailers barrels down the Trans-Canada Highway west of Hope. This particular vehicle combines the old long-nose design with some aerodynamic features. David Nunuk photo

a LNG fuelling facility and to begin using LNG-powered trucks with engine technology developed here in BC. As well, hybrid technology—gas engines combined with electric motors—has made some inroads in smaller and medium-sized trucks, though when it comes to larger highway vehicles hybrids are still in the future.

These changes were not motivated solely by concern for the environment. Back in 1973, Arab oil-producing states suddenly raised the price of their oil and banned its sale to countries that supported Israel in the Yom Kippur War. Within a few months the price of oil quadrupled, and the increase was seen at the gas pumps and in the bottom line of trucking companies. World events again interceded in 1979 when the Shah of Iran, an important oil-producing state, was toppled from power and replaced by a theocracy, and the price of oil doubled. Since that time the price of oil has gone up and down, but since 2000 the rise has been fairly steady.

The impact of rising prices on the trucking industry was profound. The improvements to engine design that had led to a decrease in emissions resulted in an increase in fuel consumption. Equally important were improvements to the aerodynamics of the equipment. When fuel costs might account for up to a quarter of a truck fleet's operating costs, no chance was lost to squeeze additional mileage out of a tank of fuel by reducing drag on the vehicles. This began in the mid-1970s in a small way with the installation of airshields on the roof of the tractor to improve airflow over the trailer. A decade later manufacturers began introducing aerodynamic styling into their new truck models.

Long combination vehicles (LCVs) are made up of a tractor pulling two full-length semi-trailers up to 41 metres overall length, but not exceeding normal weight restrictions. Proven to be safer than other equipment combinations due to strict permit conditions, LCVs are able to haul more freight in fewer trips using less fuel. Though the rig shown above is not a LCV, it is driving the Coquihalla highway, which is one of the province's permitted routes. David Nunuk *photo*

One of the earliest of these drag-resistant designs appeared in 1985 when Kenworth introduced its T600, incorporating a variety of aerodynamic features, including a set-back front axle, slope nose, cab extenders, side and roof fairings, and rounded grille and bumper. The company estimated that the new design made its trucks twenty-two percent more fuel efficient than the conventional long-nose design. Kenworth was not alone in the field; every manufacturer was convinced of the need to incorporate fuel-saving aerodynamics into their truck designs. Improvements were made to trailer design as well, with the addition of features such as side skirts and low rolling resistance tires on lightweight rims. Conventional long-nose trucks are still common, mainly in areas of the industry that do not require long highway pulls, and also with independent drivers who may be reluctant to abandon the chrome-heavy, long-nose look that for so long defined what it was to be a trucker. But for the highway haul the new drag-resistant styling has pretty much taken over.

The configuration of trailers also changed in the early 1980s with the introduction of the B-train. Like the A-train, the B-train is a twin trailer configuration but it has a fifth wheel between the two trailers instead of the conventional pintle hook attachment, making the rig easier to manoeuvre and safer on the road. B-trains are used to haul both general freight and bulk products.

As trucks and trailers have had to change, so have the drivers. Modern driver training emphasizes techniques that improve fuel economy. Progressive shifting, reducing the amount of time that the engine is idling, smoother braking and acceleration, speed control—these are all things a driver does to influence the amount of fuel used on every trip.

For motorists who share the highways with long-haul truckers, one of the more dramatic innovations of the past few years in BC has been the appearance of long combination vehicles. An LCV is a tractor with two trailers that exceed the usual legal length limit but do not exceed the maximum allowable weight (63,500 kilograms or 140,000 pounds, the same as other tractor-trailer combinations). LCVs are of two types. Rocky Mountain Doubles consist of a tractor and two trailers with an overall length of either 31 or 32 metres (roughly 102 to 105 feet) depending on the location; Turnpike doubles have an overall length limit of 41 metres (135 feet). The industry argues that the use of LCVs allows more goods to be transported in fewer trips using fewer trucks, which translates into fewer emissions being released into the atmosphere. LCVs do not operate freely on all highways but follow carefully restricted routes under strict operating conditions in only certain parts of the province. As well, drivers must meet higher standards. As of 2012 LCVs were allowed on Highway 1 in the Fraser Valley, along the Coquihalla to Kamloops and the Connector to Kelowna, and in the Peace River District from Dawson Creek to the Alberta border. As well, LCVs hauling wood chips and other mill residuals are allowed to use the Hope–Princeton Highway and the Nicola Highway between Spences Bridge and Merritt. Because of their size, the motoring public might feel intimidated by LCVs but they have been on the road in some other provinces and in many American states since the 1960s, and their safety record surpasses other equipment combinations.

....

The Teamsters Transportation Museum

For more than fifteen years a group of dedicated truck lovers have been putting their experience and know-how to work restoring a number of old freight vehicles that go back to the earliest days of trucking in British Columbia. The Teamsters Freight Transportation Museum and Archives began in the summer of 1996 when Garnet Zimmerman, president of Local 31 of the union, mentioned to Norm Lynch that he was hoping to find a 1936 pickup for the annual picnic, which was that year commemorating the Teamsters' sixtieth anniversary. Lynch tracked down the vehicle and after the picnic he came up with the idea of starting a museum. Zimmerman gave him the go-ahead to see what he could do.

Lynch knew about a bunch of old trucks, owned by the province, sitting in a warehouse in Chilliwack. They had been on display at an earlier museum in Cloverdale that had closed. Most of these vehicles had belonged to Vancouver businessman, trucker and collector Aubrey "Bob" King. King had gotten his start in the business in Vancouver in 1929 with a pair of Chevy flat decks and he had acquired a stable of companies over the years, along with a good chunk of real estate. But he shut down his freight business in 1958 over a labour dispute, and the trucks sat in the warehouse until 1974, when they came into the possession of the province. These vehicles—what one magazine writer called "King's Incredible Mothball

Norm Lynch, curator of the Teamsters Freight Transportation Museum, leans against a restored 1927 Hayes-Anderson that is part of the museum's collection. David Nunuk photo

Fleet"—formed the core of the new museum's collection. Over the years more vehicles were added until in 2011 the museum had twenty-one trucks at its facility in Port Coquitlam, some beautifully restored, others in the process of regaining their former glory.

The restoration work is all done by volunteers, as many as a dozen at any one time. Vehicles in the collection include Andy Craig's 1936 Indiana, with which he hauled over the old Fraser Canyon route to the Okanagan. When the Coquihalla Highway opened in 1986, the Indiana was the first commercial truck to cross it, with Craig at the wheel. He died the following year. The oldest truck in the museum's collection is a 1914 four-wheel drive that saw service in England during World War I before it came to Vancouver and was bought by the BC Electric Company for use as a service vehicle. Also in the museum: a 1929 White tanker truck, part of Shell Oil's Vancouver fleet delivering gas to local service stations; a 1935 Dodge Airflow that was used to deliver gasoline to Chevron stations in the Lower Mainland from the mid-1930s to the late 1940s; and a 1935 Chevrolet Maple Leaf used to haul Christmas trees in the Cranbrook area in the 1950s, along with many others.

The Teamsters Freight Transportation Museum has this beautifully restored 1936 Indiana, which is the same vehicle pioneer trucker and trucking historian Andy Craig used to haul freight between the Lower Mainland and the Okanagan in the 1930s.
David Nunuk photo

Life on the Road

Bert Wise was a nineteen-year-old sheet metal worker in Vancouver when the Great Depression struck. Unable to find a job in his trade, he decided to go into business for himself. He acquired a Ford one-ton and began picking up odd jobs around town hauling coal and wood and moving furniture; for a while he carried gasoline for Dominion Oil. In 1934 Wise moved up to a three-ton Reo, then replaced it with a Chevrolet Maple Leaf, which he used to haul lumber for the sawmills. It wasn't steady work but it was a living, and during the Depression that was something.

These four pioneers of the road were driving for Carson Truck Lines in 1951. They are (l. to r.): Bob Thompson, Bunk Seldon, Frank Allen and Darrel Derban. Courtesy of Bruce Harger

Rod Parkinson sits behind the wheel of a 1975 Kenworth V.I.T., one of the vehicles manufactured at the company's Burnaby plant. At the time, Parkinson was driving for Bill Lynch Trucking in Haney. He had started in the business in 1968 and still makes the occasional trip. Courtesy of Rod Parkinson

Wise got into distance hauling when he was offered sixty dollars to move a family from Vancouver to Oyama, south of Vernon. On the first day he got as far up the Fraser Canyon as Boston Bar. After an overnight he drove to Spences Bridge, took a sharp right turn to Merritt, then continued via Kamloops and Vernon to his destination. After off-loading the furniture in Oyama, Wise stopped at a cannery in Ashcroft on the way back to the coast and took on a load of canned tomatoes destined for Vancouver. It was the beginning of his career as a long-haul driver.

Wise started driving for White Motor Freight, an outfit that began when three friends in Merritt traded in an old car for a Model B Ford truck to haul butchered beef down to Vancouver. The plan proved to be a money loser but the company survived for several years under different ownership. After Bert Wise signed on he carried all manner of freight: honey for a beekeeper in Vernon; dynamite; oil; barrels of pitted cherries from an orchard in Summerland; wine from Calona Wines, an enterprise started in Kelowna in 1932 by a syndicate of investors that included future premier W.A.C. Bennett; general dry goods for store owners; whatever needed hauling from the coast to the Interior or vice versa. There was lots of competition as trucking seemed to be an attractive option for anyone who could drive and lay their hands on a vehicle. "We used to leave Vancouver with our gas tanks full," recalled Wise, "a forty-five-gallon drum of gas on the back end and a long piece of hose to fill the tanks with later. We packed a bar of soap, a towel, toothbrush, comb, maybe a couple of dollars, and drove all night. Next day we'd unload, reload, then try to get to bed that night. In the summer we often slept in the back of the truck."

That was the routine of the long-haul trucker during the 1930s, though pretty obviously a predictable routine was not something on which these pioneers of the road could rely.

Driving a motor vehicle is not usually thought to be a physically demanding job but in the early days of trucking it was that and more. To begin with, trips were long. It could take several days to make a run to the Okanagan and back again, depending on the weather. There was no power steering so it took a strong pair of arms to wheel a truck over the winding, rutted roads that passed for highways, and an intense concentration to watch for the multiple hazards that awaited the unwary. Suspension was minimal and the solid rubber tires had very little bounce. It was the rare driver who did not develop back problems from the constant slamming and jostling. And it was cold, at least in winter. Cabs had no heating, or defrosting. Drivers used to jam a piece of wood under the hood to keep it partly open so

Road building provided work for many men as the network of highways spread slowly through the province in the interwar years. The members of this crew are taking a rest up against their pickup truck somewhere in the Cariboo. Quesnel & District Museum and Archives P2003.2.357

Opposite bottom: A Carson Truck Lines van waits patiently for a herd of sheep to clear the highway, just one of the "hazards" likely to delay a driver in the early days. Quesnel & District Museum and Archives P1997.20.28

Left: A Mack BX gets a tow while moving a logging donkey up a steep grade near Jones Lake in 1943. Courtesy of Hank Suderman

that heat from the engine would wash up over the windshield and keep it frost-free. After stopping for the night, the last chore was to drain the radiator so that it wouldn't freeze and crack; of course, it had to be refilled in the morning. Black ice was a seasonal hazard. Drivers learned from experience to use their gears to descend a twisty downgrade instead of their brakes.

....

Once was Enough

"Many of my friends asked to ride up to Penticton and back, but it was seldom that any asked to go again. Not surprising really—what with the press of time, and the cramped conditions in the cab (you had to sleep sitting up if you were spelling the driver) and the crazy meals at odd hours, and all the work changing tires, loading and unloading, and so on. One trip was usually enough."
— *Andy Craig, trucking historian*

....

One of the hazards that faced the pioneer drivers around Vancouver was the pea-soup fog that used to blanket the Lower Mainland. "Nobody thinks of it now," recalled Frank White, who hauled freight between the Fraser Valley and the city during the 1930s. "Now if it's foggy it only means you can't go fifty miles an hour, but at the time you couldn't go five! All the traffic came in on Kingsway and before Fraser Street you'd start running into low spots. Bloody huge fog banks. You'd follow the streetcar tracks right downtown and you'd develop a kind of sense where you should turn... Your horn wasn't any use because nobody would know where it was coming from. We'd have to hire kids to go in front of us, to lead us through the fog in some of the worst spots. Lead us with flashlights and hollering. You couldn't see anything. A lot of the kids would come down to Water Street, around the truck depot, on a real foggy day just for that job. Usually you'd give them two-bits or so to get you out of there... Those fogs have disappeared now, but they were just yellow mud. I ran into a streetcar once and there was absolutely nothing that I saw until I hit it."

Changing a tire was no easy job and early truckers usually had to do it themselves. Here J. Wise, a driver for Carson Truck Lines, tackles the inside dual while D. Foster looks on. Quesnel & District Museum and Archives P1997.20.53

Shovel and Shift

"On a typical run from Vancouver to Bridge River we had no sleep and no meals. All we did was shovel snow and shift gears. I was a passenger on many trips when, due to road conditions, we were stopped for ten to twelve hours at a time. It always amazed me how my husband [Albert Wihksne] travelled so smoothly, negotiating each and every curve. He made fantastic time considering the [Fraser] canyon was a virtual trail back then compared to today's superhighway."
— Harriette Wihksne

In these early days every wheel twister had to be his own mechanic. There was no one to come to the rescue if a tire blew or an engine broke down. Bert Wise recalled one trip when he lost the crown and pinion gears in his rear end outside Yale in the middle of the night. He stopped the first motorist to come along and asked him to shine his headlights on the truck so he could remove the rear end. Wise hitched a ride with this good Samaritan down to Vancouver, where he got the gears repaired, then returned to the canyon to reinstall the rear end. He figured that in sixteen months of running between Vancouver and the Okanagan he replaced fourteen axles and about sixty tires. Drivers were paid by the trip, not the hour, so any delay was costly. In the 1940s a round trip to the Okanagan usually earned the driver $22.50.

The job involved much more than simply driving. Drivers loaded and unloaded the freight manually. Most vans were of the stake and rack type, meaning they had removable side racks that had to be

In the winter there was little or no snowplowing. Drivers had to dig their own way through the drifts, and trips to the Interior could take several days as a result.

Quesnel & District Museum and Archives P1997.20.97

Andy Craig poses with his famous Indiana loaded with freight at Spences Bridge in 1938. Those are two chesterfield suites on the roof, bound for a Penticton furniture store.

Courtesy of John Wihksne

A vintage Johnston Storage truck does a wheelie in downtown Vancouver in 1927, drawing a crowd of curiosity seekers. It looks like the load of pipe was too heavy and too far back and lifted the front of the truck right off the ground. The second truck is coming to the rescue.

City of Vancouver Archives
CVA 99-1974, Stuart Thomson
photo

covered with tarps and roped down to protect the freight from the elements. Often this was done more than once as cargo was picked up and dropped off along the way in a practice known as way-freighting. Andy Craig explained: "Way-freighting wasn't much fun in the worst seasons of the year, when we were fighting miles of unploughed snow, or in the spring break slugging through gumbo. It still makes me shudder to think of those stops in deep winter, when you dropped out from the heat of the cab and into the shock of freezing weather, then the trip around to the tailgate, and frozen ropes, and the tarp stiff as a piece of steel. Before you got the tarp on the roof, and sorted through the load for the pieces to be delivered, then wrapped everything up again and collected monies due, and got the waybill signed, your fingers would be so stiff and chilled that for miles after you would be sitting first on one hand then on the other to bring back the circulation—and man, how they would hurt! And meanwhile you were still trying to shift gears and keep the rig on the road, and thinking 'Damn the way-freight!' You modern drivers are lucky; you don't have a clue what it was like."

Accidents were an inevitable part of the job. Most involved delays and repairs but some were more serious. In October 1937, on a night when the road was icy and a heavy fog had moved into the Fraser Canyon, Fred Carson, founder of Carson Truck Lines out of Quesnel, missed a turn at the top of the hill just north of Boston Bar and plunged down the embankment. The truck smashed into a tree and Carson was crushed beneath the weight of his load coming down on top of him.

In a rare kind of accident, the oil line on this truck caught fire on the Hope–Princeton Highway and before Herb Reddecopp, the driver, could put it out his fire extinguisher ran dry and the vehicle and its load of lumber were destroyed. Courtesy of Brad Reddecopp

Grabbing Forty Winks

"You would drive until there was no way you could stay awake any longer and then you would pull over, but you'd leave the windows in the cab open, so you didn't sleep too long. The cab was only four feet wide and even with your knees drawn up you were so uncomfortable you couldn't sleep for long—and to be dead sure you didn't sleep for long we did most of our sleeping at Boston Bar, near where the trains roared by, so the noise would wake us up. The winter was better in that you couldn't oversleep, it being so cold. The truck would stay warm enough for an hour and then you'd wake up stiff with cold."
— *Andy Craig, trucking historian*

The dangers and the discomforts ensured a strong camaraderie among the drivers. At many spots in the Interior the roads were so narrow that two trucks could not pass. When vehicles met, one had to back up to the nearest pullout to allow the other to go by. As they passed the drivers would roll down their windows to share a cigarette and some gossip before moving on. (Those narrow roads spooked more than one motorist. Gil Cornish, who drove the route in the 1940s, often met tourists who were too frightened to chance the highway—there were no guardrails, remember—and paid him twenty-five

Above: This photograph originally appeared in Weekend Magazine *in 1963, accompanying a story about the perils of driving the Alaska Highway. Norman Arnott (l.) has stopped to help another trucker dig himself out of the ditch.*

Left: During World War II Albert Wihksne, shown here, was hauling logs for the gold mine at Bralorne, winding his way along the narrow Bridge River roads in his battered 1937 Diamond T.

Courtesy of Hank Suderman; courtesy of John Wihksne

109

Top right: Many of the original Cariboo roadhouses made the transition to the motoring age. 70 Mile House, for instance, remained in business until it burned in 1956.

Right: The Hunter Creek service station was a popular spot for truckers once the Hope–Princeton opened. That's a very early auto hauler parked in front.

Bottom: A postcard shows the Alexandra Lodge in the Fraser Canyon near Chapman's Bar.

Royal BC Museum, BC Archives C-07672; Courtesy of Trudy Jarvis; Courtesy of Bruce Harger

dollars to freight their car down to Hope.) When a truck broke down the next one to come along always stopped to offer help or give a tow into the nearest town. Drivers were in competition but they were also members of the brotherhood of the road. Most of them knew each other and socialized when they stopped for gas or laid up at one of the truck stops for a coffee, a meal or a bed.

Then, as now, drivers had favourite spots to pause along the route. Some of these places traced their origins back to the original roadhouses that were built to accommodate travellers on the old Cariboo Wagon Road. These crude log buildings were built every fifteen kilometres (nine miles) or so and took their names from the distance (in miles) beyond Lillooet. So, for instance, 70 Mile House, which was built in 1862 to house the original road builders, remained in business well into the trucking era until it burned down in 1956. One of the favourite truck stops on the Fraser Canyon route was the Siska Lodge, south of Lytton, operated by the Gaugh family. It burned down in the mid-1960s. Another spot was Alexandra Lodge near Chapman's Bar, where the proprietor kept an outdoor goldfish pool stocked all summer with bottles of pop cooling in the water. Passing truckers were welcome to drop a nickel in a tin and take one. The Alexandra Lodge survives in the twenty-first century as a private residence.

While service stations were few and far between, an important oasis was Walter Harrington's garage in Boston Bar. "Cog" Harrington, who died in 1979 at the age of sixty-six, is a legend in the BC trucking industry. He opened his service station, Harrington Motors, in the mid-1930s and came to the rescue of countless trucks and buses that ran into trouble on the canyon route, using his snub-nosed Ford tow truck to haul disabled vehicles out of ditches and snowbanks. Harrington, who wore a patch over an eye that was injured when a cable snapped during one of his highway rescues, was the founder of the "Cog Grinders Club." The club was restricted to truckers who had driven 100,000 accident-free miles through the Fraser Canyon. Privileges of membership included accommodations at the hotel he operated in Boston Bar, and access to its swimming pool and beer parlour. Harrington wrote a regular column in *Motor Carrier* magazine that was part folksy industry gossip column, part political rant. A typical item

Siska Lodge

"Nearly all the trucks stopped at Siska, and the lodge gave us special treatment. We could always go downstairs and find coffee at any hour of the day or night, and if any of the Lodge people were awake they would cook up whatever we asked for. In the cooler they had everything from bacon and eggs to the biggest steaks you ever tried to wrap yourself around. These steaks were always over an inch thick, and so big you had to have your vegetables on the side, because there was no room left on the platter. For cooking this (perhaps at one a.m.) they had the nerve to charge all of a dollar and a half, and if you wanted to sleep the balance of the night they could always find a bed someplace in the Lodge and only add a dollar to the bill. So you can see why all the early drivers had a soft spot for the Gaugh family, and won't forget them."
— *Andy Craig, trucking historian*

Above: Driver Bunk Seldon parks his Carson Truck Lines van at Siska Lodge sometime in the early 1950s.

Left: Walter "Cog" Harrington at his Boston Bar garage in 1942, before the accident that cost him an eye. The truck is of the pre-war tarp-over variety.

Photos courtesy of Bruce Harger

A crowd of freight trucks lined up at Cog Harrington's place in 1938. The drivers are inside wolfing down some of Cog's delicious grub. Courtesy of Rod Parkinson

from September 1969: "I am calling on Premier Bennett to give Phil Gaglardi his cabinet job back as Minister of Highway as soon as possible. Let's get things rolling again. I would suggest you don't give Phil any more jet planes [Gaglardi had been forced to leave the cabinet the previous year following charges that he'd used a government jet to fly relatives] but get him a new Public Works dump truck with air conditioning and all the jazz, and make him go up the Yellowhead Route and find out when the road is gonna be open. We would all like to know." Harrington particularly disliked Jake brakes for the noise they made and in his magazine column he awarded a "stink pot of the month" award to drivers who used them going through Boston Bar. In 1986 a new bridge across the Fraser north of the community was named for him.

Scaling Jackass Mountain in the 1950s

"It was winter in 1958 or 1959 and I was offered a chance to take a ride with a fellow who was taking a load to Salmon Arm. We went to Hope and then we turned and went up the Fraser Canyon. It was snowing and it was a little slippery. 'Our worst place,' the fellow told me, 'will be Jackass Mountain. Because of the grade, and because you can't get a run at it, and because if somebody spins out they'll block the road and that means we

have to stop. And if we have to stop, that means we have to chain up.' Then he told me that if we had to stop, I had to hop out of the truck, grab the hydraulic jack out of the box and throw it in behind the drive wheels. Otherwise, we'd start sliding back down the hill. Well, we started pulling Jackass Mountain and a car spun out up ahead of us and one truck stopped and we had to stop. As soon as we came to a stop, I opened the door and hopped out on the road and I went flat on my butt, 'cause it was black ice. But I got the jack out and started walking back alongside the truck as it starts to slide back down the hill. I got behind the rear duals, it was a tandem truck, threw the jack in behind the tire, and that was enough to stop that whole load from going down the hill. Then we chained up and as soon as it was clear we went up over the hill. But I wouldn't have believed until that day that you could slide a commercial tandem truck trailer, fully loaded, with good equipment on it, back down a hill. That was Jackass Mountain!"
— Frank Linke, trailer mechanic

....

For all its dangers and discomforts, driving truck was still an exciting occupation for young men in the pioneer era. "Coming from a small town to drive truck around the city, well that was *living* as far as I was concerned," reminisced Frank White, who hailed from Abbotsford. "What does a young fella want anyway? Just to keep roving and wrestling things up. I hauled into Vancouver for nine years steady, 'til 1941. I drove close to a million miles on that job. But I don't know... I liked it." Bert Wise agreed. "Every trip something different happened," he wrote. "I've picked rocks off the road, nearly been wiped out in a slide, driven through floods, pulled guys out of wrecks, towed cars and shovelled snow. But we were young and didn't think of ourselves as heroes. We were out to make a buck and all the hazards were just part of the job."

Top left: This view of the Cariboo Road shows mule teams and wagons on Jackass Mountain north of Yale. Ever since, the steep hill has been a landmark for drivers using the canyon route.

Above: Oops! A driver failed to negotiate the Siska Bridge in the canyon, leaving his Hayes in need of a rescue and himself in need of a stiff drink.

Royal BC Museum, BC Archives A-03879, Frederick Dally photo; Courtesy of Kevin Duddy

Trucker Poet

Charlie Docherty from Quesnel used to haul freight in and out of the Cariboo. Among his many talents, Docherty fancied himself a bit of a versifier. Here is an extract from one of his poems about the Fraser Canyon route:

This road is rough, and trucks are tough,
And the drivers are the same;
For the load is heavy, and the road is
    long
On this trail of Cariboo fame
With its thousand curves and its
    thousand hills,
And bridges and creeks galore;
The rocks roll down from the hills above
Clear down to the Canyon floor.
You can hear the hum of the motor,
Echoed back from the rocks and glades,
And your engine boils, and you sweat
    and cuss
As you climb its heavy grades.

The Nishiama brothers, Jim on the right and George on the left, both drove for Carson Truck Lines. Courtesy of Bruce Shantz

World War II played a significant role in consolidating the importance of the trucker to the economy. During the war, drivers were in high demand since many young men had enlisted in the armed forces. In 1941 Parliament declared trucking to be an essential service and as a result drivers could not be conscripted. Supplies of fuel, tires and engine parts became increasingly scarce on the home front as they were needed for the war effort. Truckers received ration books for fuel; if they ran out they could apply for more coupons but they had to be able to prove their need. In order to conserve, rival carriers began pooling their cargo, and deadheading—returning from a delivery with an empty truck—was avoided whenever possible.

Canadians had it driven home to them how important trucks were to the successful prosecution of the war and this enhanced public image spilled over into the postwar period. Then, in August 1950, the country experienced a nine-day nationwide rail strike. Doomsayers predicted that without rail freight the economy would grind to a halt, businesses would fail and many people would lose their jobs. Instead truckers stepped in and filled the gap, working around the clock all across the country to handle essential freight, with the result that there were no major shortages. After the strike ended, many shippers decided to switch permanently from rail to road. It had become apparent just how vital a healthy trucking industry was to a healthy economy. Until the strike, wrote Arthur Hailey, who would become a bestselling novelist but at the time was editor of *Bus and Truck Transport* magazine, "the Canadian trucking industry was not really recognized as a national entity, but it was recognized then in a hurry, and remained so ever since."

The war had accelerated improvements to truck technology and these continued through the 1950s. Enclosed vans replaced the stake and rack trailers. Sleepers were common, power steering made its

Running to Catch Up

"Millar and Brown had teams running between Vancouver, Trail, Cranbrook, Calgary, and Edmonton using conventional Kenworths. These things had 36-inch sleepers with crawl-through and inside they were dark as a whale's tummy. One smokin' hot August afternoon a pair of drivers heading east swapped places at the bottom of Sherman Pass in Washington State. The guy coming off shift decided to straighten the blankets on the bed and, just as his rump touched the door latch, the tractor bounced sharp left. The sleeper door popped open, the guy fell backward onto the road. He got up, dusted himself off, found he only had a few scratches, then tried running after the truck but he was barefoot, the asphalt was hot and the rig was picking up speed. Finally, out of breath, he stopped and waved like crazy but the rig kept right on going.

"So there he was, stranded in a foreign land on a remote stretch of highway, no identification, barefoot, wearing only an undershirt and boxer shorts. It was not looking good. A few minutes later a big black Oldsmobile 98 rounded the corner with two little old ladies. They stopped when he stuck out his thumb. 'Where are you going young man?' 'I fell out of my truck and my partner is a few miles ahead. Do you think you can catch him?'

"'Oh sure, sonny, hop in, we'll find your truck.' They roared up the hill and found the truck nearing the summit. The driver said, 'Keep going, I'll get out at the top.'

"The last pull up the Sherman Summit has a steep pitch near the top so our man hid behind a boulder 'til his rig lumbered past. As it went by he trotted alongside, jumped on the running board, swung into the cab, then crawled into the sleeper. His gape-jawed companion asked, 'Where've you been?' 'Don't ask and don't wake me.'"
— *Ted Campbell, former driver*

Millar & Brown ran freight trucks between Cranbrook and the coast. Unlike the rig in the story, the one in the photograph does not have a sleeper. If the driver wanted to rest, he either had to catch forty winks in the cab or pull in at one of the truck stops along the route. For many years it was impossible to drive across southern BC without having to detour down through Washington for part of the trip.

Courtesy of Dietmar Krause

During World War II just about everyone jumped on board the Victory Bond bandwagon, including the Pacific Meat Company, which decorated its trucks with publicity for the bond drive. *City of Vancouver Archives CVA 586-1171, Don Coltman/Steffens Colmer photo*

These vehicles belonging to Wood & Fraser Transport stood idle on Vancouver's Alexander Street during the war because they could not get gasoline to operate. Fuel, tires and engine parts were all in short supply during the war. *Courtesy of Gordon Hay*

appearance and cabs started getting heaters, but drivers still sat on bench seats and handbombed the freight. At the same time, improvements to the highway system meant that life on the road was less perilous for long-haul truckers.

Truckers faced an important upgrade to their licence requirements in 1971. Up until that time, for-hire drivers of commercial vehicles were known as chauffeurs and were required to obtain a chauffeur's licence to handle most vehicles on the road. Bruce Shantz, who drove for Chapmans Freight Lines for many years, recalled that when he started working in the Vancouver warehouse loading freight in the late 1950s the drivers took him out at lunchtime to teach him how to handle the diesel tractors. When he felt ready, he went down to the licence office, paid a fee for a chauffeur's licence, no test required, and as simple as that he was a professional driver. The C licence was a small metal tag that many drivers attached to their caps or their belts. In 1971 the new system introduced classified driver's licences. Drivers had to prove their ability to handle particular types of equipment—for example, tractor-trailers, heavy trucks or buses—in order to obtain a particular classification of licence. There were six classifications. The three most relevant for the commercial driver were Class 1 for semi-trailers, Class 2 for buses and Class 3 for trucks with more than two axles.

During World War II, with drivers in high demand and short supply, women had entered the profession for the first time. Though trucking remains a male-dominated business—a 2004 study showed that less than three percent of truck drivers are female, compared to about forty-seven percent of the labour force—an increasing number of women are entering the profession. One of them, Angela Jones, who drives for Ken Johnson Trucking in Langley, was influenced by a trucker father to get into the business herself. Her father, Frank Reid, drove for Arrow for many years and often took his young daughter along with him on trips. Now a seventeen-year veteran behind the wheel, Jones insists that trucking

Above: On longer runs it was common for drivers to work in pairs, known as sleeper teams—while one man drove, the other caught up on his sleep. That's Micky McLaughlin in the bunk and Hank Cochrane behind the wheel of a cab-over Hayes in the early 1960s. Note that the instrument panel is above the driver's head in this model rather than on the dashboard. Courtesy Tony Gussie

Left: Times have changed for the better, as this interior of a brand new Kenworth shows. David Nunuk photo

Container trucks make the run to and from Deltaport. Container drivers form their own specialized part of the industry. Most are owner-operators and they require special passes to enter the port facilities.

David Nunuk photo

is a good job for a woman "because it is not a real physical job, it's more checking on safety and doing things properly and dealing with the public. I see a lot more women drivers out there now. When I first started people would see me in the truck and they'd turn around and give me this big thumbs-up and smile and point. They were just so surprised." Nowadays, says Jones, the public seems to agree that truck driving is an acceptable job for a woman. That acceptance does not necessarily extend to the male driving fraternity, however. Shirls Leclerc, an owner-operator who drives for Berry & Smith Trucking in Penticton, reports that the hardest part of the job has been dealing with the antagonistic attitudes of other drivers. "Women aren't really accepted that well out there," she says.

Another Ken Johnson driver, Ingrid Giesbrecht, recalled that when she became a driver in 1979, delivering freight with a tractor-trailer around the Lower Mainland, she knew of only one other woman driving in town and it was very difficult. She recalled the sexism of some of the male drivers: "I had a couple of guys who made my life miserable. I used to come home in tears almost every day for the first six months." The abuse only stopped when, without her knowledge, a few of her co-workers took the two offenders aside and warned them off. "The customers were never the issue. They'd be, 'Oh, it's a girl!', and everybody would be standing on the loading dock staring at me. You don't know how much more difficult that made it, where you're just learning; it was so stressful. But the customers all welcomed you with open arms."

For Ken Johnson, Giesbrecht hauls chemicals and other tanker cargo, some of it hazardous material. At times she has to suit up from head to toe in rubber gear, with full face shield and goggles. "It's a good job for anybody but you can't be a girly girl and do it," she admits. "You can't be worried about your fingernails and your makeup and whether or not you've got calluses on your hands or you're going to get dirty. Of course you're going to get dirty. Fifteen minutes after the day has started, you can write your hair off. Hat hair, you're done! If little things like that bother you, well it's not the profession for you."

Before 1971, a Class C chauffeur's licence was all someone needed to drive a commercial truck. It came with a small metal tag, like these, which most drivers attached to their belts or caps. Courtesy of Christopher Garrish

A Job and a Husband

"In 1979 I was dating a truck driver. It was our third date and he phoned to cancel because he had a chance to run down to Seattle hauling a container. He said, maybe you want to come along. I thought, sure, sounds like fun. I worked for a freight-forwarding company at the time. So I went along on the one trip and at the end of the trip I thought, 'I can do this, I think this would be great.' So I went to Whalley Driving School the very next day. I asked the guy what I had to do and he told me I had to get my air brake ticket first. So I booked that for the weekend and I did my theory Saturday–Sunday. The following week I went in and took my first three-hour lesson. The next day I went back for my next lesson and the guy told me 'I can't let you waste any more money.' 'Why, I said, do you think I'm that bad?' And he said 'No, you're a natural.' I booked my road test for Friday, less than two weeks after I'd made the initial decision to go drive. I went for my driving test and did well. I was so excited I grabbed the guy by both ears and gave him a big smooch right in the middle of his bald forehead.

"I went back and told the guy I was dating and he said, 'No woman I'm dating is going to be doing a man's job.' So I said, 'Well, it's a good thing we're not seeing each other anymore.' And that was the end of him.

"The only trucking company I knew was the company that came in to pick up our trailers where I worked. That was R & G Trucking. So I went over there pleased as all get out and said 'Here I am, I've got my licence, hire me.' He looked at me and said 'I don't like to hire people right out of driving school but it would be interesting having a woman working here. I'll make a deal with you. You come in on the weekends and drive around with my weekend driver and if he says you're okay, you're on.' The weekend driver is now my husband; we've been married for thirty-three years. So it worked out good. I got a new job and a husband to boot."
— *Ingrid Giesbrecht, Ken Johnson Trucking*

Who says it's no job for a lady? Angela Jones,
a driver for Ken Johnson Trucking in Langley,
has been behind the wheel for eighteen years.
David Nunuk photo

Still, the failure of women to enter the profession in significant numbers is an issue within the industry, which is concerned about a shortage of drivers generally. The need to be absent from home for long periods and the physically demanding nature of the work are two factors that continue to discourage women. "I just don't think women have been brought up thinking that driving tractor-trailer is something they should be doing," says Giesbrecht. Yet for her it has been a good career. "After all these years of driving I'm actually surprised that there's not more women doing the job."

About twenty percent of all drivers belong to a union; it is often the Teamsters, though recently the Christian Labour Association of Canada has become more active. The International Brotherhood of Teamsters was formed in the United States in 1903 when two other unions of drivers and freight handlers merged. Over the years it has organized drivers in various aspects of the trucking industry, including freight drivers, dairy tanker drivers, film industry drivers and so on. In 1976 the Canadian Conference of Teamsters was formed to cater to the specific needs of the union's 74,000 Canadian members, and during the 1990s the CCT changed its name to Teamsters Canada. Since 2001 Teamsters Canada has been an autonomous organization with affiliations to the IBT. In BC, Teamsters Canada has four locals: Local 31 for general freight; Local 155 representing workers in the film industry; Local 213, which was created in 1946 and today represents workers in a broad variety of industries; and Local 464, the oldest local in the province, formed in 1919 for workers in the dairy industry.

The BC trucking industry was not heavily unionized until the 1960s. And since that time labour disputes have troubled the industry from time to time. Indeed, in 1967 the executive secretary of the Automotive Transport Association, the forerunner of today's BCTA, described the need for better management-union relations as "desperate." In October 1970, the ATABC, representing the carriers, sat down with the Teamsters to bang out a new contract and when talks failed drivers walked off the job the following February. Members of the ATABC retaliated by locking out unionized drivers before negotiations resumed and a contract was attained. Then, in the spring of 1976, the scenario was replayed. Owners were facing escalating labour costs at the same time as they were dealing with the impact of the fuel crisis. The result was another strike/lockout.

During this period carriers negotiated agreements with their unions on a sector-by-sector basis. Companies operating in a particular sector—log haul, construction, bulk freight, whatever—in a particular region adhered to these master agreements. But this system was abandoned in the 1980s in favour of each company making its own contract agreement with its union.

One of the bitterest labour disruptions occurred during the summer of 2005, when the approximately one thousand container truck operators serving the Port of Vancouver staged a withdrawal of services. This was not the first time that the owner-operators who constitute the majority of the container fleet had tried to force improved payment. Following a five-week work stoppage in 1999, collective agreements were signed establishing increased rates of compensation for owner-operators. However, gains made from this agreement were soon eroded and on June 27, 2005, members of the newly organized Vancouver Container Truck Association serving terminals at the Vancouver Port Authority and the Fraser River Port Authority (the two combined with the North Fraser Port Authority in 2008 to become a single agency, now called Port Metro Vancouver) again withdrew services, disrupting port operations and threatening the regional and national economies. (The port dispute came on the heels of a work stoppage earlier in June by about a thousand dump truck drivers in the Lower Mainland. For two weeks the drivers refused to service construction sites until an agreement was hammered out, giving them a twelve percent fuel surcharge on top of their regular rates.) Container truck operators complained that while costs of operation were rising, especially the cost of fuel, the trip rates they received were not.

As the task force appointed to look into the dispute reported, "significant pressures had developed which made it difficult for owner-operators to maintain reasonable incomes." Other grievances related

Following pages: The vast facility at Deltaport, south of Vancouver, is Port Metro Vancouver's largest container terminal, handling about seventy percent of the containerized cargo that passes through the port. David Nunuk photo

to the operation of the dock facilities. The dispute highlighted how important a smoothly functioning port system is to the health of the economy and how crucial the container truck sector is to that system. At the time, trucks were carrying about thirty percent of the containers coming into the ports and sixty-three percent of the export container traffic, with rail handling the rest. The Port Authority estimated that trucks were carrying $30 million worth of goods in and out of the port every day. Large regional exporters, such as the BC forest industry (which exported seventy percent of its product in containers), were particularly concerned at the prospect of a prolonged stoppage. With the help of a facilitator appointed by the federal government, the dispute was resolved on August 4 after the drivers received pledges of improved compensation levels from the trucking companies that hired them. (The drivers later affiliated with the Canadian Auto Workers.)

A fuel truck roars up the Sea-to-Sky Highway in the early morning hours. David Nunuk photo

One of the most significant developments in the trucking industry since the 1970s has been the emergence of the owner-operator (also known as a lease-operator). The earliest drivers were owner-operators in the sense that they owned their own trucks, but modern owner-operators are drivers who contract out their services, and their equipment, to a company. The trend was encouraged by the recession of the early 1980s, and by 1998 one in five drivers in Canada was an owner-operator (about 5,500 in BC). Using contract drivers allows companies to adjust quickly to changing demand for their services and to save on the expense of buying and maintaining a fleet of vehicles. For their part, owner-operators appreciate the independence of being one's own boss, even though some may work consistently for the same employer. A Statistics Canada study in 2000 indicated that owner-operators may pay a significant price for their independence. The study found that compared to company drivers, owner-operators on average work longer hours per week but earn lower after-tax incomes. Some companies use owner-operators exclusively; others use a mix of contract and company drivers; others use only their own employees. For-hire carriers use a higher percentage of owner-operators than private companies; nationally, about a third of the drivers in the for-hire sector are self-employed as opposed to only three percent in the private sector. As well, highway drivers are more likely to be owner-operators than local, city drivers.

Jobs in trucking have been transformed in the past couple of decades. At the same time as it has become physically more comfortable, driving has become more complicated. It is not an unskilled job. The equipment is more sophisticated and the responsibilities are more varied. Long-distance drivers wheel the big rigs across the continent; local drivers travel within the province, perhaps within a city, dropping off freight and meeting customers; specialized drivers handle flat decks, tankers, containers

Pallets of freight are being loaded into a trailer at the Cold Star Freight Systems warehouse in Victoria. David Nunuk photo

Jack Vleeming, a veteran driver with Clark Freightways, approaches China Bar Tunnel in the Fraser Canyon on his regular route to Prince George. David Nunuk photo

and bulk loads and usually need particular training. Drivers are responsible for cargoes that might be worth hundreds of thousands of dollars and moving it along a public highway system that is full of risks. And the driver is only one member of a team of people who keep the trucks running safely and on time. Mechanics, dispatchers, computer programmers, IT specialists—they all play a role in delivering timely service for the best possible price.

....

Road Warriors

"It wasn't that long ago [during the 1960s] that guys were going over Highway 3 with 225 horsepower engines pulling thirty-five-foot trailers, maybe 70,000 pounds. Now here we are asking the driver to marshal 140,000 pounds at about twice the speed up and down over the Coquihalla. In some ways it's easier, but the responsibility and the challenges are every bit as high for these guys today, at the speeds they're travelling and the loads they're carrying."
— Mal Shephard, Detroit Diesel

....

A major challenge facing the industry is a labour shortage dating back at least to the mid-1990s. At the turn of the new century Paul Landry, then president of BCTA, estimated that in BC the industry was short "hundreds" of drivers, and that some companies were turning away business for lack of trained personnel. When asked by *Motor Truck* magazine to state the top priority for the industry, Landry identified the shortage of qualified drivers. "There is a lifestyle associated with long-haul trucking that would not appeal to many people today," he explained. "Drivers have to be away from home and family for long periods of time. The freedom of the road appeals to some people but not to everybody. So we've had trouble attracting our fair share of women, for example; we've had trouble attracting our

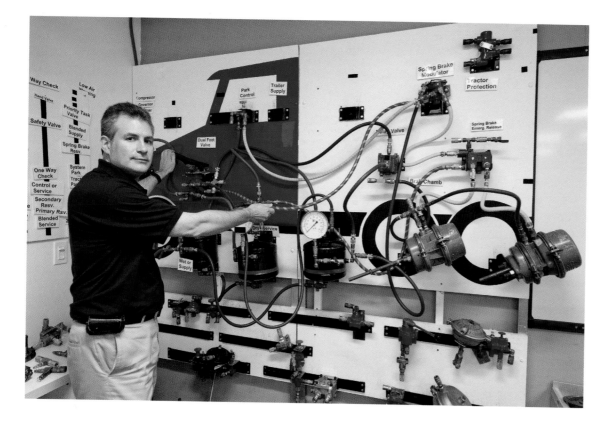

fair share of young people." Not only are young people not attracted to the industry, but the trucking workforce is markedly "grey." In 2003 a study showed that a disproportionate number of employees in trucking were forty-five years old or older; in other words, approaching retirement age. A provincial industry that requires 5,000 new Class 1 drivers annually is getting less than 2,500. And this is not just a local issue. In 2011 the American Transportation Research Institute identified the driver shortage as number three on its list of top ten concerns facing the industry.

A related issue is the high rate of "churn," or turnover, experienced by employers. About eighty percent of new drivers leave their first company within a year and many of them leave the industry altogether. To address the challenge of attracting people to the industry and then also retaining them, BCTA in 2007 launched an Industry Strategic Human Resources Plan. Among other things, the plan proposed improvements in driver training standards, training for smaller companies in how to attract and retain employees, and plans to promote a career in trucking to non-traditional audiences (for example, women and aboriginal peoples). The overall aim is to improve the experience and skills of entry-level drivers and to promote trucking as a career, not simply a job.

Trucking does appeal to certain communities more than others. According to Sabik Singh, whose family has been in the dump truck business in BC since the 1940s, Indo-Canadian immigrants began to enter the industry in increasing numbers at the end of the 1970s. It was relatively easy to acquire a licence and little formal education was necessary. And as the number of South Asian drivers grew, with heavy concentrations among dump truck drivers and container haulers, it was easy for others to make the connections within the community to find work. During the upswell in public concern about truck safety that occurred in the mid-1990s, some people placed the blame on Indo-Canadian drivers in particular, arguing they were poorly trained and dodging the safety rules to keep company profits up. Sabik Singh felt his community was being unfairly maligned and responded to the criticism by creating the Southern BC Truckers' Association to help drivers in the dump truck and aggregate hauling sectors

understand safety standards and government regulations, and to lobby for improvements to vehicle safety and driver training. Still, the popularity of trucking among some immigrant groups has not made up for the shortfall of trained drivers generally and it is an issue that continues to concern the industry.

Opposite: A Canadian Freightways rig heads toward the Fraser Canyon south of Spences Bridge. David Nunuk photo

....

Being the First

"In 1948 I was hauling blacktop for the Trans-Canada Highway in Rosedale, ten miles east of Chilliwack. This was the year that I applied for my motor carrier plate, called the H plate. This was used in order to be able to haul aggregates and other commodities within the Greater Vancouver area, including the Fraser Valley. When I went to the Motor Carrier Commission office in Vancouver to get the licence, I was told that I was the first East Indian trucker to make application for hauling."
— *Sabik Singh, G.H. Singh & Sons Trucking*

....

There is a widely held view among trucking professionals that truck driving suffers from a poor public image. Even a generation ago, driving was a respected profession. Today truckers seem to have slipped in public esteem. Trucking is associated in the public mind with unsafe practices, a lack of education and poor working conditions. "It is a challenging environment, particularly the long haul, and it is not suited to everybody," admits George Lloyd, retired now from a long career in the industry. "You're away from home and the conditions aren't always very good. Outsiders don't always see trucking as an attractive career." And it can be a high-stress job, having to cope with the dangers of adverse weather conditions and the frustrations of traffic congestion.

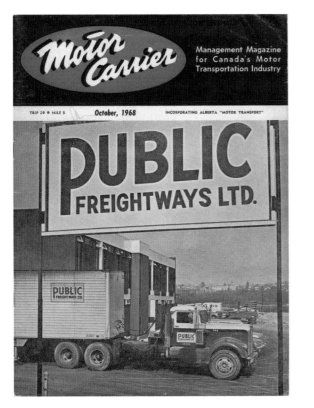

Above: Herb Reddecopp (with the accordion) and his brother Phil operated one of the earlier trucking companies in Abbotsford. They are shown here at the family garage in 1957. Courtesy of Brad Reddecopp

Far left: For many years Motor Carrier Magazine was a forum for the industry.

Left: Larger companies had their own in-house magazines. This is a copy of the Johnston Journal, published by Johnston Terminals for its employees. The cover shows kids taking part in a sack race at the company picnic.

Courtesy of Harvie Malcolm; courtesy of Dietmar Krause

A dump truck makes its way along the Upper Levels Highway in West Vancouver. During the 1990s the dump truck side of the industry was a flashpoint for public concerns about highway safety, leading to changes in driver licence testing standards and higher penalties for failing to adjust brakes. David Nunuk photo

Still, for those who like it, they like it a lot. The job offers independence, variety and a chance to show personal initiative. Remuneration compares favourably with other occupations. This was not always so. In 1991 a Statistics Canada study indicated that truck drivers were the worst paid of employees in the four transportation sectors: truck, rail, maritime and airlines. However, wages had improved by the new century and more recent data shows that people in the trucking industry are compensated at a comparable if not higher level than employees in other occupations requiring similar credentials and experience. To the extent that driving is failing to attract new recruits, it does not seem to be income level that is the determining factor.

For many drivers trucking is as much an obsession as a profession. Take John Wihksne, for example. He started driving in 1961 at a hydroelectric project in Manitoba and among other things drove long haul to California and ran a driver training school before he retired. "When I was in high school," he says, "a couple of guys at West Van High when they graduated drove gravel trucks on the North Shore and they'd come by the school and, oh wow, I thought that was a wonderful thing. The truck thing was just an obsessive thing through my whole life. I tried other things. I worked for the telephone company, I was a meat cutter, I sold, I did all kinds of things. But I couldn't shake this truck thing."

Ultimately the lure of the road—"the bug" as long-time Prince George driver Mel McConaghy calls it—remains a bit of a mystery. "People get the bug to drive truck in different ways, and for different reasons," McConaghy writes in his memoir, *My Life Through a Broken Windshield*. "Some people follow in their father's footsteps. Others are standing at the side of the road one day when a big, shiny, chrome-encrusted, smoke belching monster goes thundering by and they're smitten. Still others realize that it's a way of making a decent living without having a bunch of letters behind your name. Sometimes the sense of power, or the thought of being in control of a 139,000 pound unit roaring up and down the highway through mountain passes and city traffic while manoeuvring an outfit that's 83 feet long, can result in 'King of the Road' syndrome. I'll never know for sure why truckers do what they do, but we do it. I don't know how many people I've asked why they drive trucks, and nobody's ever been able to give me a definitive answer."

This Peterbilt truck and trailer hauled for Pacific Inland Express (P.I.E.).
Courtesy of Kevin Duddy

All in the Family

Today there are about 23,000 registered trucking companies in BC. The majority of these outfits are small to medium-sized operations hauling general freight for their customers. Others work in the natural resource industries or in construction, hauling products in bulk or carrying heavy machinery or specialized loads. Each of these diverse companies has its own story. Telling them all would fill several books. This chapter profiles a few of the carriers to show how they managed to carve out a business for themselves in the highly competitive trucking industry.

The Victoria Baggage Company, forerunner of Victoria Van & Storage, had its original headquarters in this warehouse on Fort Street in Victoria. It is the 1920s and the company has made the transition from horse-drawn wagons to "modern" motor trucks. Courtesy of Victoria Van & Storage

Often these companies trace their origins through two or three generations of family ownership, all the way back to the early days when carriers made the transition from horse-drawn wagons to motor freight in the World War I era. In Victoria, for example, Waldo Skillings and a partner formed the Victoria Baggage Company in 1908 and took on the contract as the official cartage agent in the provincial capital for the Canadian Pacific Railway. One of the company's wartime assignments was to transport the delicate pieces of the huge telescope that was being installed atop Little Saanich Mountain as part of the new Dominion Astrophysical Observatory. It was the largest telescope in the world at the time and every bit of it was moved by horse and wagon. At war's end Victoria Baggage, based on Fort Street, retired its teams of horses and made the switch to motor trucks. When Waldo Sr. died in 1938 his three sons took over. While one of them, Waldo Jr., went into politics—first as a Victoria alderman, then as a leading figure in W.A.C. Bennett's Social Credit government—his brothers Frank and Stewart managed the business. During World War II the company got into heavy hauling for the shipbuilding industry and on the household moving side became a member of United Van Lines. In the 1950s the name of the company changed to Victoria Van & Storage and a third generation of the Skillings family got involved. Fuel distribution became another specialty and by the 1980s the company had the largest fleet of tankers on the Island. In 1991 Bob Skillings bought out his three brothers and along with yet another generation of young Skillingses he began a process of streamlining operations for the new, economically unregulated, highly competitive era. Today, more than a century after its founding, Victoria Van is known as a household moving specialist and a heavy industrial hauler.

Not many carriers can claim a lineage going back four generations of the same family, as the Skillingses can, but family ownership has always been a characteristic of the BC industry. In Vancouver a good example of a long-established family business is Arrow Transport. One of the earliest cartage companies in the city, it began operations in 1918 as Kitsilano Auto Express with founder Chuck Charles using a Model T half-ton to move people to Kitsilano. By 1922 Charles had acquired a fleet of six trucks and renamed the company Arrow Transfer. Six years later he merged with one of his rivals, Claude Bouchard, and became Arrow Transport. Today the business, Arrow Transportation Systems, still managed by members of the Charles family, is one of the province's largest heavy-haul companies serving the resource industries.

Waldo Skillings Sr., shown here in 1933, founded Victoria Baggage as the official cartage agent for the Canadian Pacific Railway. Courtesy of Victoria Van & Storage Co. Ltd.

An Arrow Transfer low-bed moves a house through the streets of Vancouver in February 1950. Vancouver Public Library 81147A, Artray photo

Carrying baggage and parcels was the way a lot of small companies got into the cartage business. Vancouver Trunk and Bag got the message across by making its vans look like actual trunks. This Federal model is crossing the Georgia Viaduct in 1926. *Vancouver Public Library 543*

BC Rapid Transit, a subsidiary of the BC Electric Company, operated a freight line in the Fraser Valley from 1924 to 1932. This Federal model truck, towing two trailers, departs the company's New Westminster depot. *Royal BC Museum, BC Archives C-02470 Dominion Photo Co. photo*

The trucking industry has consisted of an impressive variety of operations, from this small package handler in Vancouver in 1935 (l.) to a heavy-duty ore-hauling tractor at Cominco's Sullivan Mine in Kimberley in 1944 (below) to a giant Hayes-built vehicle hauling coal for West Canadian Collieries during the 1940s. *Vancouver Public Library 10690, Leonard Frank photo; Royal BC Museum, BC Archives B-05334; City of Vancouver Archives CVA 1184-1999, Jack Lindsay photo*

Right: The driver of this old Merchant's Transport vehicle would have had to load and tie down all the freight himself.

Below: An Arrow Transfer crew moves a power shovel to a work site in Vancouver in June 1935.

Courtesy of Dietmar Krause; City of Vancouver Archives CVA A18528, Stuart Thomson photo

At Christmastime in 1969 Arrow undertook one of the oddest heavy hauls in the history of trucking in the province. It began when a group of killer whales, or orcas, swam into Pender Harbour, about seventy-five kilometres (forty-seven miles) northwest of Vancouver, where a couple of local fishermen captured them behind a net by spreading it across the mouth of a small bay. Killer whales were in high demand at the time for public display, and when the fishermen put out the word that they had some for sale buyers from all the major North American aquariums hurried to Pender Harbour to take a look. Five of the animals were sold to aquariums in California but one was purchased by a pair of young animal collectors from Vancouver who were acting on behalf of a French buyer who wanted a killer whale for a marine park he was building in Antibes. After paying the purchase price of $16,000, the young entrepreneurs, Robin Best and Chris Angus, were faced with the challenge of transporting their purchase, a 5.5-metre (18-foot) female they christened Su-san, down to the Vancouver Airport, where they had arranged to put her aboard a transport plane for Europe. Angus approached Arrow to take on the job. He found some fabricators to build an aluminum cradle to go on the back of a flatbed. The plan was to bring the whale down from Pender Harbour suspended in a canvas sling inside a vinyl bag held by the cradle, all on the back of the truck. Ice water would be sprayed over the animal during the trip to keep its skin wet and cool.

Three days after Christmas a crew hoisted Su-san aboard the Arrow flatbed with a crane and off they went on a fifty-kilometre (thirty-mile) drive down the Sunshine Coast Highway to the ferry terminal at Langdale. Everything went according to plan until the truck started down the steep hill leading into the town of Gibsons. The vehicle's compressor gave out and with it, the air brakes. Chris Angus later recalled what happened. "I can remember starting down the hill and I guess the driver had the emergency brake on... because the brakes were smoking. The vehicle was picking up speed and it was in first gear and the clutch was smoking like... wow, there's all this smoke pouring out. Robin and I were on the back with the whale, standing with the whale. Halfway down the hill before the hairpin the driver gets on the running board and is steering the truck and yells at us, 'If she starts to roll, go off the high side.'" But they made it safely down the slope and onto the ferry in one piece and managed to get the compressor working again. In Horseshoe Bay a police motorcycle escort met them and they rolled the rest of the way to the airport without any mishaps. The whole adventure gave new meaning to the industry motto: "If you got it, a truck brought it!"

※

Prior to World War II there weren't many large carriers in BC. The industry was dominated by small owner-operators, many of whom had begun operations during the Depression when all it took to set up a haulage business was a used truck and bit of gumption. As pioneer trucker Bert Wise observed, in the dirty thirties "it seemed like everybody was getting into the act."

One of these intrepid entrepreneurs was George Williams, a young Vancouver man who had to borrow the fifty dollars he needed to start his own business. It was 1929 and Williams used the loan to buy a four-door Dodge touring car. Removing the back seats, he installed a box and started hauling antique furniture for Love's Auction House. This was the beginning of Williams Moving & Storage, which is still in business as a moving specialist today, more than eighty years later.

In 1953 Williams became one of the founding members (now the largest member) of United Van Lines, a network of moving companies that operates across North America. When Williams purchased Robertson Moving & Storage in Calgary in 1971, it became the largest privately owned operation of its kind in western Canada. That same year George Sr. died and his son, George "Sonny" Williams, who

Following pages: Arrow Transfer began in the household-moving business with this fleet of vans, shown in 1929. City of Vancouver Archives CVA A17431, Stuart Thomson photo

Sonny Williams was learning the business from the ground up when he posed beside one of the company moving vans in 1948. Courtesy of Williams Moving & Storage

Williams Moving & Storage, now one of the largest moving companies in Canada, began in this small Vancouver warehouse, shown in 1945. Courtesy of Williams Moving & Storage

had joined the company when he was sixteen years old, took over. It was under Sonny's leadership that the operation expanded from a couple of branch locations to several offices in BC and Alberta. As part of this expansion, Williams took over all distribution in western Canada for Sears. Suffering from ALS (Lou Gehrig's disease), Sonny died in 1995. He was succeeded by his son Jim, meaning that Williams has been managed continuously by members of the same family for its entire history.

Over the years, family-owned operations like Williams, Victoria Van and Arrow have been prominent not just in the Lower Mainland but around the province. And they still are. Take City Transfer, for example. Based up the Sunshine Coast in Powell River, it began as a local cartage company in 1920. The operation changed hands several times before Bert Long and a couple of partners bought it in 1947. Eventually Long took full ownership of the company. In 1980 he sold it to his son Harold, who expanded operations significantly, adding a barge service and extending the range of the freight service along the entire Sunshine Coast and down to Vancouver. Harold's children have since taken the reins of the business.

Another carrier with family ties, and roots farther north, is Bandstra Transportation, based in Smithers. It was founded in 1955 as Smithers Transport by John Bandstra Sr., a recent immigrant from Holland. Trucking was in his blood—his father owned a trucking company in Europe—so it was no surprise that John got into the business. Along with one of his brothers and a third partner he purchased a local freight operation. Originally there were two Internationals hauling groceries and general freight to Prince Rupert and back along the mud track that passed for a road in those days. Until some of the wrinkles were taken out of the road in 1967, the company could only use a nine-metre (thirty-foot) trailer because some of the turns were too tight for anything larger. On one of the early trips the truck and driver ended up in the Skeena River. "They said it was the brakes," John Bandstra says, "but maybe it was his eyesight." The company hauled milk overnight to Prince Rupert, made regular runs to Kitimat where Alcan had just completed its aluminum smelter, and eventually expanded into household moving, low-bed hauling and carrying supplies to the various mines in the area. Almost sixty years after its founding, Bandstra Transportation Systems Ltd. is still headquartered in Smithers and several members of the family are still involved.

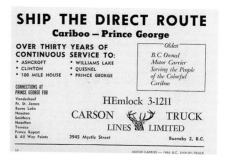

A Carson Truck lines business card offers
freight services for "the Colorful Cariboo."
Courtesy of Hank Suderman

The re-opening of the Fraser Canyon Highway in 1927 sparked the appearance of the first long-haul companies in the province. They are too numerous to mention each by name but several of these pioneer operators stand out. Fred Carson was a Barkerville storekeeper who expanded into freighting in the mid-1930s in order to obtain goods for his store from Vancouver. Subsequently he moved to Quesnel where Carson Truck Lines hauled between Prince George and the coast and as far west as Fort St. James. When Carson was killed in an accident in the Fraser Canyon his licence was picked up by another driver, Les Cotter, who ran the company under its original name until it was taken over by creditors in 1949. George Wood, formerly a partner with Alex Fraser in his own Cariboo trucking firm, was installed to manage Carson Truck Lines (he later bought the operation) and made such a success of it that the company prospered, moving to a new terminal in Burnaby in 1958. When Wood finally retired in 1973 he sold the company to All-Trans Express Ltd., marking the demise of one of the best known and most durable firms from the pioneer period.

Another of the early companies was Lee's Transport, started in 1924 by Sam Lee, who had migrated west from the prairies with the idea of prospecting for gold. Instead he settled in Vanderhoof, acquired a Model T truck and went into the haulage business. In 1931 his son Ebert made the company's first run down to Vancouver using a three-ton Model B Ford and inaugurating Lee's Transport's regular service to the coast. During the war, Lee's had the contract to haul into the Pinchi Lake mercury mine. Located

Lee's Transport and Carson Truck Lines were
two of the main companies using the Fraser
Canyon route during the 1940s and 1950s.
These drivers are taking a break somewhere in
the Cariboo in 1942. BC Trucking Association

These vehicles belong to three of the Interior's pioneer companies: Western Freight Carriers based in Revelstoke, Lee's Transport in Vanderhoof and Hustons Cariboo Transport in Williams Lake. Courtesy of Kevin Duddy; Courtesy of Kevin Duddy; Courtesy of Dietmar Krause

A brochure advertises the services of Northern Freightways, "serving the land of opportunity." Courtesy of Kevin Duddy

just north of Fort St. James, it began producing mercury in 1940 for use as a component in wartime arms manufacturing. Lee's hauled fuel, lumber and equipment from the railway at Vanderhoof up to the mine site and brought the mercury back out. It was carried as a liquid in flasks about a foot tall and the same in diameter. Each flask weighed between thirty-six and forty kilograms (eighty and ninety pounds), recalls Jake Wall, who drove the Pinchi Lake run for Lee's. "On a K7 International if we had six or seven rows just above the wheels, we were loaded." Nowadays, of course, mercury is considered a highly toxic substance, but at the time the drivers were in constant contact with it. "Every once in a while I'd sweep the mud out of the cab," says Wall, "and there'd be pieces of mercury the size of a quarter rolling around in there and I used to roll that out and save it in a beer bottle. And we used to play with that mercury, rub it between our fingers. When they started talking about mercury poisoning I used to wonder how I never got poisoned!" Lee's grew into one of the largest freight companies in the Interior, with a fleet of twenty-eight trucks travelling south to Vancouver and all the way to Dawson Creek in the Peace River country. After the war Wall briefly drove the Vancouver to Prince George run for the company. "The Vancouver trucks were the elite of the crew," he explains. "Ebert supplied the drivers with white coveralls with their names on them, and Lee's Transport emblazoned on the back." In the mid-1950s Lee's merged with Northern Freightways, a Dawson Creek outfit.

Northern had an interesting history of its own. It was founded by Roger Forsyth, one of the civilian workers who had come north to Dawson Creek in 1942 with his own truck to work on the construction of the Alaska Highway. As the war ended he purchased two more trucks and started Roger A. Forsyth Trucking. After beginning as a lumber and coal hauler, Forsyth and his partners soon were handling freight of all types on the new road between Alberta and Alaska. This was the beginning of Northern Freightways. The company was the first to offer a scheduled general freight service between Edmonton and Dawson Creek. "Roger was always ready to haul anything, large or small," said one of his drivers. A big expansion happened in 1951 when Forsyth purchased fifteen Mack trucks to handle gravel

hauling for Westcoast Transmission during construction of its natural gas pipeline to southern BC. In 1954 Northern inaugurated a trailer-on-flatcar service on the PGE Railway to Vancouver, making it a pioneer in piggyback in BC. When this service ended two years later, Northern became partners in a Vancouver–Dawson Creek run with Carson Truck Lines, exchanging trailers at Prince George. By 1958, the year Forsyth sold to Canadian Freightways, Northern had a fleet of seventy-five vehicles and 150 employees.

Down in the southeast corner of the province, Millar and Brown was a Cranbrook-based outfit that appeared toward the end of World War II. It was founded by Walter Millar and his brother-in-law Fred Brown. Starting with three trucks and an operating authority that confined them to the Cranbrook area, the company expanded to start a Vancouver route via Idaho and Washington. By the time Millar retired in 1975 the operation was one of the largest in western Canada, with a fleet of 450 vehicles—reefers, dry vans and flat decks.

The map on the side of this Northern Freightways semi illustrates the wide swath of northeastern BC that the company served.
The Exploration Place, Wally West Collection

Some Famous Characters

"There were some famous characters in those days [the 1930s]. There was Knobby King of White Motor Freight. There was Porky Parkinson, Ken Pollack who had one of the first English Gardiner diesels on the road. They wouldn't start in the cold weather so they built a bonfire under the crankcase every morning to start them. I'll never know why the whole outfit never burnt up."

— Walter "Cog" Harrington

As this advertisement illustrates, Millar and Brown expanded from its base in Cranbrook to serve routes across western Canada and into the northern US. Courtesy of Hank Suderman

These are advertisements for just some of the companies that carried freight between the coast and the Prairies in the 1950s.

Courtesy of Hank Suderman

It is a long way from the highway to the backcountry, which is where many independent truckers made a living contracting their services to the logging companies hauling from the cut to the dump or down the road to the sawmill. Of all these small-time operators the most famous was Bill Schnare, a mechanical genius who worked out of a garage in Abbotsford. "As far as I know the man who showed the logging industry how to use trucks was Bill Schnare," says Frank White, who worked for Schnare and spent many years driving logging trucks himself. The story goes that sometime in the mid-1930s Schnare repossessed a Ford three-ton and not knowing what to do with it allowed his teenage son Stan to take it log hauling. When the venture turned a profit, Bill converted a few more old Fords and S & S Trucking was in business. "He anticipated whole generations of seat-of-the-pants mechanics," writes logging historian Ken Drushka, "whose happiest moments were spent staying up all night, deep in the bowels of a hard-used logging truck some contractor needed to have on the job in the morning." The Schnares came up with innovative solutions to all kinds of problems involved in cutting the steep slopes of the Fraser Valley and Harrison Lake, and before long they were in demand by the big logging companies on Vancouver Island.

In 1938, just as Schnare had secured his reputation for working wonders with old trucks, he went out and got himself four brand new fifteen-ton Macks, the largest trucks that had ever been used in the woods to that time. Most people in the industry scoffed at the idea of using such heavy vehicles on the makeshift roads, but once again Schnare proved the know-it-alls wrong. The Macks handled bigger loads than anyone had seen before and by their example showed that trucks could replace railways in the woods. By 1950, the year the Schnares sold their company, they were the largest independent log haulers in BC.

Bill Schnare, the Abbotsford garage mechanic often credited with spurring the changeover from rails to roads in BC logging, chats with the driver of one of Schnare's state-of-the-art Macks on Vancouver Island.

Courtesy of Hank Suderman

A crew loads logs onto a flat deck truck at a logging show somewhere in the Cariboo. The driver will need all his nerve to manoeuvre the load down that narrow plank road to the mill.

The Exploration Place, Anderson Photographic Collection

Not all logging companies used contractors for their trucking needs. Some, like Herb Doman, branched out into the business themselves. For all his success in the forest industry, Doman's roots as a businessman were actually in trucking. Born in Duncan, the son of Sikh immigrants, he began selling sawdust and firewood from a dark green second-hand Dodge truck when he was just a teenager. In 1955 Doman Industries incorporated as a trucking and home supplies retailer. Soon he was building sawmills and acquiring logging rights all over Vancouver Island. Through acquisition Doman ended up in control of an industry giant, today's Western Forest Products, with annual revenues in the hundreds of millions of dollars.

The basis of his empire was lumber, but Doman also expanded his trucking business, Doman Transport. It may have begun with a single used Dodge but soon the company was adding flat decks and semi-trailers and hauling lumber and business supplies across the strait to the Vancouver area, as well as servicing the Island logging industry. In 1964 Doman purchased Marpole Transport, a flat deck operation based in south Vancouver. Marpole had been carrying loads of pipe to the Island and had worked out an arrangement with Doman to backhaul loads of lumber, so the two companies had a working relationship that made the amalgamation a smooth fit. As Doman Marpole Transport, the new company played a role in the construction of several BC megaprojects, including the Coquihalla Highway and the Bennett Dam, and extended its service throughout BC to the Yukon and into the western US.

During the 1980s Doman decided to get out of trucking and concentrate on his forest operations. A group of managers with Doman Marpole, including brothers Pudge and Sarge Bawa, who had begun as drivers with the company back in the mid-1950s, put an offer together and in 1991 took over the operation. The group also included a third brother, Shub Bawa, who had been an executive with Johnston Terminals and its subsidiary Public Freightways. The new owners changed the name of the Island operation to Trans-Isle Freightways while the Vancouver company (now based in Delta) reverted to the original Marpole Transport name. The company, still run by members of the Bawa family, hauls across western Canada and into the northwestern US using a fleet of 175 tractors and 300 trailers, including flat decks, tankers and chip trains.

A 2007 Freightliner SD hauls a trailer for Marpole Transport, based in Delta.
Kevin Oke photo

Van-Kam Freightways, based in Surrey and one of the largest carriers in the province, has been in business for sixty-five years and counting. David Nunuk photo

The 1950s brought an upsurge in the Canadian trucking industry due in part to its response to the national rail strike (see chapter four). In BC this was followed by the resource boom of the 1950s and 1960s, which saw expansions in mining, forestry and hydroelectric development on an unprecedented scale in the province. Prosperity naturally brought with it an increased demand for fast, efficient transportation, which meant enhanced opportunities for truckers. This was the period that saw the creation of several companies in the Interior, including Berry & Smith in Penticton and Van-Kam Freightways in Kamloops, companies that are among the industry leaders today. By 1965 there were 144,000 commercial vehicles registered in the province, an increase of 30,000 vehicles in just five years.

One Interior carrier that took advantage of the postwar economic boom was Chapmans Freight

Berry & Smith began operations in Penticton in 1958, hauling fruit for local customers. The company also provides local bus service.
Berry & Smith Trucking Ltd.

Chapmans was another Okanagan-based carrier. As the vintage vehicle suggests, the company dated back to 1919 when it started out as a passenger service between Kelowna and Penticton. Courtesy of Dietmar Krause

Top: An International belonging to Lee's Transport needs a tow to get it out of a ditch at Cottonwood Hill near Quesnel.

Below: Walter "Cog" Harrington's Ford tow truck rescued many stranded truckers during the interwar years. Harrington advertised himself as "Canada's Most Modern Wrecking Service."

Courtesy of Kevin Duddy; Courtesy of John Wihksne

5 | All in the Family

Lines. Starting out in 1919 as a stage line carrying passengers between Kelowna and Penticton, it expanded into local pickup and delivery, carrying the mail and serving as the Kelowna agent for Shell Oil. With the opening of the Hope–Princeton Highway in 1949, Chapmans began hauling to the coast, first of all as a household goods mover and then carrying general freight. During the 1960s the company began running tractor-trailer outfits through the Fraser Canyon and was one of the principal carriers making regular runs between Vancouver and Prince George. In 1966 Canadian National, which was looking for a trucking operation to service Brenda Mines near Peachland, purchased Chapmans. The company continued to operate its general freight service to points throughout the Interior, first under CN and then, from 1977 to 1993, under the Motorways banner.

The 1950s saw a dramatic merger that brought together nine separate operations into a single company, the largest merger in the provincial trucking industry to that time. The story begins in 1928 with the arrival of Jimmy Vanderspek, a nineteen-year-old immigrant from Holland who had come to BC to join his elder brother John in Princeton. Young Vanderspek got hold of one of the early Hayes-Anderson vehicles and began hauling coal from the mines around town. One thing led to another, as it so often does in the trucking business, and before long he was down in Vancouver operating what was known as a butter-and-egg route, buying produce from Fraser Valley farmers and selling it to retail outlets in the

city. From there he purchased a five-ton International Harvester and began hauling canned fish from the Fraser River canneries to the Okanagan. This was the beginning of Vanderspek Transportation and before long he had as many as a dozen trucks running from his depot at Broadway and Carolina Street to Kamloops, Kelowna and Vernon via the Fraser Canyon route. He was often behind the wheel himself, usually accompanied by his wife, June. "I can remember when there was a young broken-down Cog Grinder by the name of James Vanderspek," recalled Cog Harrington, "he used to drive up and down the old Fraser Canyon like a fiddle string and quite often he used to have his beautiful young wife June Vanderspek riding with him. Everyone just used to love June, and of course we all had to like Jimmy a little bit because he was her husband. But ninety percent of the deal was June."

In the Ditch

"In the early days the big job wasn't to pay for the truck, it was to keep the truck on the road. Many of the truckers, especially Jimmy Vanderspek and his outfit, spent more time over the bank than on the road. Between black ice, snow slides, [and] washouts, it really was quite a deal."
— Walter "Cog" Harrington

A Public Freightways rig makes an appearance at Expo 86 in Vancouver. From 1951 to 1989 PF was one of the premier freight haulers in the province. Courtesy of Dietmar Krause

Right: This West Coast Freight Company reefer is taking on a load of refrigerated freight in the mid-1960s. WCF was a Vancouver Island company that became part of the Johnston Terminals empire. Courtesy of Dietmar Krause

A fleet of Johnston Terminals COEs (cab over engine) lined up at the company's Cambie Yard on southeast False Creek in Vancouver in the early 1960s. Courtesy of Dietmar Krause

Johnston Terminals transshipped freight from across Canada and around the world.

Top: A Johnston truck picks up freight at the Vancouver docks during the 1950s, obviously before the age of containerization.

Left: Johnston had an air division, the first in Canada, offering air freight forwarding to Vancouver from Toronto and Montreal. Trucks like this one in 1964 picked up the freight for next-day delivery.

Photos courtesy of Dietmar Krause

151

By the middle of the war, gas and rubber rationing forced Vanderspek to suspend his freight business and he converted his trucks for airport construction on Vancouver Island. But once the war was over he got back into freight hauling and in 1951 he engineered the merger that would transform Vanderspek Transportation into Public Freightways Ltd. Chief partner in the new arrangement was Gordon Winton of Winton's Transfer, a family business originating in Abbotsford. Winton became manager of the new operation, but the merger involved a total of nine companies, most of them centred in the Fraser Valley. The newly organized Public Freightways, with terminal facilities in Kamloops and Princeton as well as from one end of the Fraser Valley to the other, was the largest short-line haul company west of the Great Lakes. Along with its freight operations, the company had a tanker fleet, a heavy-haul division and was the exclusive contract carrier for a variety of customers, including the Fraser Valley Milk Producers and Granby Mines. Public Freightways flourished for twenty years, steadily increasing its range to the Kootenays and the Cariboo. By 1968, when PF opened a new, eight-acre headquarters terminal in Burnaby, it had 400 employees and a fleet of 58 tractors, 63 straight trucks, 60 trailers and 35 flat decks moving over three million kilograms (seven million pounds) of freight weekly. Growth was expensive, however, and not necessarily profitable. Faced with the challenges of increased operating expenses, Public Freightways merged with Johnston Terminals in 1971, though it continued to operate under its own name.

Johnston was another local company that began as a horse-and-wagon outfit just prior to World War I and evolved into a transportation giant. Elmer Johnston began hauling furniture through the streets of Vancouver in 1913 when he incorporated the Johnston Storage Co. Johnston purchased his first gas-powered motor vehicle four years later. The postwar period brought steady growth; he added a warehouse operation and in 1927 merged it with the cartage business as Johnston National Storage. Not long after Elmer Johnston died, in 1949, the company was purchased by a Winnipeg outfit named Security Storage, which sold it in turn in 1953 to a group of Vancouver businessmen. The new owners

created a public company, Johnston Terminals & Storage, and embarked on another period of expansion. Because of the nature of the provincial licensing system (see chapter seven), it was simplest to expand by buying out the competition and during the 1960s Johnston purchased several companies servicing different parts of the province or engaged in different kinds of hauling. The nerve centre of its expanded operation was the Cambie Yard, a huge warehouse/shipping facility on False Creek at the south end of the Cambie Street Bridge.

In 1971 Johnston was purchased by a group of its senior executives, backed by the Bank of BC, in partnership with Versatile Cornat Corporation, a Vancouver company. This arrangement lasted until 1978 when the management group purchased the other half of Johnston Terminals from Versatile Cornat. The 1980s turned out to be a decade of unprecedented challenges. The company, which employed more than 1,800 people and had annual revenues of $92 million, ran into a perfect storm of difficulties, including a recession, continental deregulation of the industry and increased competition. When cost-cutting measures failed to turn the business around, the company was forced to begin selling off, or closing down, its divisions. In 1986, for example, the furniture moving division, Johnston Moving and Storage, familiar to generations of homeowners and office managers, was sold to Allied Van Lines. Then, in March 1989, Public Freightways, which had been steadily downsizing, went out of business. Finally, in 1992, what was left of Johnston Terminals closed its doors.

Railways and trucks have long been rivals in the business of freight forwarding. For decades railways had enjoyed a monopoly in the freight business and they were not happy to see the upstart trucking industry begin to encroach on their dominance in the years following World War I. During the

Building a Train in the Sky

Johnston Terminals had a number of divisions, one of which was Johnston Heavy Haul, which billed itself as "The Heavyweight in Heavy Haul." One project that helped solidify this reputation was the construction of the SkyTrain transit system in Vancouver in 1984. The SkyTrain features lightweight railcars running on their own guideway elevated above street level. The erection of the guideway was a mammoth task. The rail ran on precast concrete beams suspended between steel-reinforced concrete pillars. The initial line from New Westminster to downtown Vancouver required more than a thousand of the beams, each weighing about 100 tons. Johnston designed its longest flatbed unit ever, a thirteen-axle steering dolly capable of carrying beams 33 metres (108 feet) long. Using six of these massive dollies, Johnston began hauling the beams from a plant in Richmond to the rail line construction sites. The haul began on the first day of 1984. Every morning at two a.m. the convoy of six rigs, each carrying a beam, set off through the dark, pre-dawn streets along a carefully selected route with a police escort and pilot cars. At the site, large cranes lifted the beams and positioned them atop the pillars. This was the routine for nine months until the job was done.

Opposite: Merchant's Cartage was a heavy-haul specialist that eventually joined the Johnston Terminals stable. Here one of its flatbeds transports a pair of steel girders to a construction site in the 1950s. Courtesy Dietmar Krause

In March 1958 the moving and storage division of Johnston Terminals undertook what was billed as "Canada's Largest Office Move." BC Electric, the utility company that had also operated Vancouver's streetcars, was moving head office from its former headquarters building at the corner of Carrall and Hastings, opened in 1912, to a new office tower at Burrard and Nelson. Three years later the provincial government nationalized BCE and formed BC Hydro, a crown corporation. Thereafter the new headquarters was known as the BC Hydro Building. Large moves like this one were coordinated like military campaigns and called on all the company's vast resources.

Courtesy of Dietmar Krause

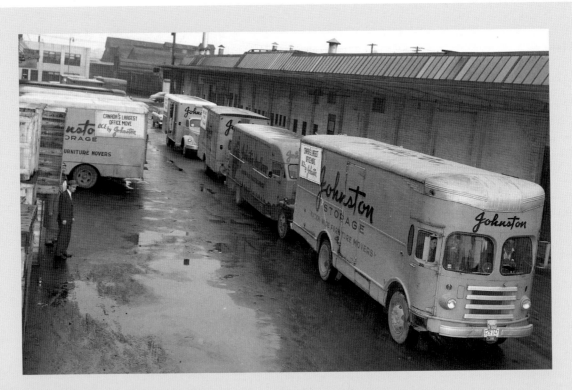

Depression, as freight revenues declined, the railway blamed truckers for their problems and petitioned the federal government to rein in the industry. For their part, truckers believed that the government was giving preferential treatment to the railways in the form of subsidies and favourable regulations. During the national rail strike of August 1950, the trucking industry had impressed the public with its ability to keep the economy moving and during the 1950s trucks began to overtake rail as the most important form of land transport. In BC it was also an era of extensive highway construction. As a result, the railway companies decided the time was right to get into trucking themselves by buying up existing carriers. The most important of these purchases nationally was in 1957, when the Canadian Pacific Railway bought Toronto-based Smith Transport, the largest transport company in the country. (Canadian National also was involved in trucking but on a less ambitious scale.)

In BC, Canadian Pacific became a major presence in the industry, and its wide-ranging role can be charted by following the career of George Lloyd. Lloyd began working for CP in 1951 in Kamloops, where he started as an eighteen-year-old swamper on the night shift, unloading freight from trains. Before too long he was driving CP Express delivery trucks around town. In 1960, CP organized CP

Merchandise Services, a merger of CP Express with several trucking companies it had bought, including Expressway Truck Lines, OK Valley Freight and Cascade Motor Freight. Lloyd undertook a series of moves to manage operations in different regional centres. By 1969 he was in Vancouver as operations director with what had become CP Transport. In 1975 CP Transport reorganized into six divisions, one of which was CP Bulk Systems, and Lloyd was asked to take charge. Over the next fifteen years he built the division into a $40 million operation. But with deregulation and company reorganization, Canadian Pacific decided to get out of trucking and in 1990 it sold Bulk Systems to Alberta's Trimac Transportation. Lloyd had intended to retire but instead he stayed on with Trimac as head of the newly named Trimac Bulk Systems, focussing exclusively on hauling wood chips. Lloyd ran the company until 1997, when he finally made good on that threat to retire.

Jim Clark, founder of Clark Freightways, poses beside one of his early reefer vans. Clark started the company in the mid-1950s and for a while he was a one-man show, driving between the Lower Mainland and the Okanagan several times a week.

Clark Freightways/Greg Rogge

With improvements in refrigeration technology during the 1950s came an increase in the volume of frozen and fresh meat and produce being carried over the road. One operator who took advantage of this new opportunity was a driver named Jim Clark, who in the mid-1950s decided to go out on his own mainly transporting produce from the Okanagan down to the Lower Mainland. In 1959 Clark Transport obtained a licence to haul frozen foods, which became the core of the business. Three years later the company changed its name to Clark Reefer Lines and began operating from a terminal in Burnaby, hauling all kinds of perishable freight on a less-than-truckload basis. During the 1980s the company expanded its delivery area west from Prince George all the way to the Queen Charlotte Islands. Since its expansion to Vancouver Island in the 1990s, the company, which became Clark Freightways, now serves almost the entire province. While it does haul a lot of dry freight, its fleet of eighty power units and close to two hundred trailers focus on temperature-controlled LTL freight for a range of food-related businesses: grocery stores, produce and dairy companies, restaurants and wholesalers. Like so many BC companies, Clark Freightways is a family affair, with the founder's son, Marcus Clark, taking over management of the company from his late father.

A fleet of COEs lines up at the old Clark Freightways warehouse in Burnaby in the mid-1980s. Today the company headquarters is located in a new facility in Coquitlam.

Clark Freightways/Greg Rogge

In the Beginning

"He [Jim Clark] was a one-man show for the first few years. His brothers who were firemen, Paddy and Peter, they would pitch in and make the odd trip to give him a hand. He started off hauling produce from the Okanagan. If there was anything he could put on to get up there, great, but the backhaul was really his head haul. By the mid-1960s he had moved into a little two-bay warehouse on Boundary at First Ave. My mom was a part of the company in the early days, doing the bookkeeping and payrolling and whatnot. By about 1969 we had moved into our old building on Norland Avenue. By that time we were running a few trucks in town, doing pickup locally for out-bound freight, and a single line haul truck pulling out of town. Nowadays we call it a peddle run. Dad would drive up there and make the deliveries and pick up the produce and come back."
— *Marcus Clark, Clark Freightways*

Another Lower Mainland company that managed to dodge the pitfalls of deregulation and increased competition was Argus Carriers Ltd. Argus began early in 1948 when founder Gerry Royston, just back from the war, was looking around for a way to make a living. Using a small loan, he managed to purchase an Austin truck, which he parked outside Spencer's department store on Hastings Street. When he saw

Since it was incorporated in 1955 as a small parcel service, Argus Carriers has grown into a major freight carrier serving the Lower Mainland, Vancouver Island, the Thompson–Okanagan and the US Pacific Northwest.

Courtesy Rod Neufeld, Argus Carriers

a woman having trouble carrying her parcels he offered to deliver them to her home for a twenty-cent fee. When she agreed, his parcel service was up and running. Within a few months Royston had a second truck and a first employee. Growth continued and in 1955 Argus Carriers was incorporated. Initially specializing in small parcel delivery around Vancouver, the company steadily expanded and by 1972, when it was purchased by Rey Neufeld, the fleet consisted of sixteen small trucks. Under Neufeld and his son Rod, who acquired the business from his father in 1997, the company took on larger freight and acquired larger vehicles, expanding to the Island and the Interior. It also struck up a relationship with Peninsula Truck Lines in Washington State, which made Argus an international carrier. Today its fleet of trucks and vans carries dry freight of all kinds around the Lower Mainland, up the Fraser Valley, to the Thompson–Okanagan and into the American Pacific Northwest.

Much of the trucking industry consists of for-hire carriers like the ones discussed in this chapter. These are companies for which carrying freight is their main business. Another important branch of

the industry consists of so-called private carriers. These are companies whose primary business is not trucking at all—it might be manufacturing, operating restaurants, retailing groceries or any number of other enterprises—but which operate fleets of trucks to transport their goods. Large beverage companies like Coca-Cola and Pepsi fall into this category. A smaller example is Paradise Island Foods, a Nanaimo-based food manufacturer and distributor of cheese and other food products. Instead of hiring out the delivery of their products, Paradise Island maintains its own fleet of Kenworth tractors and refrigerated trailers. Closely related to the private carrier is the for-hire carrier that only hauls for one customer. McDonald's, for instance, uses Martin-Brower to transport the supplies for all their restaurants, while Commercial Logistics Inc. in Richmond provides trucking services almost exclusively to the beverage industry.

The one thing that all these various companies have in common—private, for-hire or somewhere in between—is that they all belong to BC's diverse trucking family.

Based in Langley, Triton Transport is the largest heavy haul company in BC. One of its recent challenges was to transport one of the world's largest cranes into BC Place for the installation of the stadium's new retractable roof. Courtesy of Triton Transport

Truckers Get Organized

I n the decade immediately before the outbreak of World War I, Vancouver was a city of boom and bust. First came the boom—"the golden years," as Alan Morley called them in his history of the city—a period of sustained economic growth based on the Klondike gold rush and the opening of the Canadian West. The 1911 census showed that Vancouver had become the fourth-largest city in Canada and was gaining on third-place Winnipeg. The following year the value of building permits approached $20 million. Banks, warehouses, hotels and residences were all part of the construction boom. The

This fleet of Studebaker vans made deliveries for Calladines Groceries in 1918. It was companies like Calladines that had come together to form the General Cartage and Storage Association in pre-war Vancouver. City of Vancouver Archives CVA A17657, Stuart Thomson photo

city was served by two major rail lines with a third, the Canadian Northern, nearing completion. In 1909 the Canadian Pacific Railway, the city's largest landowner, showed its confidence in the future by beginning work on a leafy subdivision of mansions for the super-rich. Named for Thomas Shaughnessy, the company's president, the carefully designed neighbourhood was dubbed "CPR Heaven" and quickly became Vancouver's most fashionable address. At the same time the Dominion Trust Company built a new headquarters on Hastings Street that at thirteen storeys was the tallest building in the British Empire and a symbol of the energetic optimism that pervaded the city, and the province.

Then came the bust. During 1913 the local economy plunged into recession. The British investors who had financed much of the boom withdrew their money, fearing the outbreak of war in Europe. The value of real estate dropped like a stone. Construction stopped. Businesses failed and the sidewalks were crowded with the unemployed as they looked for jobs. Even the Dominion Trust Company went bankrupt. Vancouver, the Terminal City, looked to be terminally ill.

It was in this year of unrest and uncertainty, 1913, that a group of freight handlers in the city, some of them horse-and-wagon men but some of them operators of a new motor truck or two, got together

By the 1920s business in Vancouver had recovered from the war and cartage companies like Hapman's Motor Service, with its small fleet of Federal trucks, were thriving.
Vancouver Public Library 559

By 1948, when these members met in convention in the Hotel Vancouver, the industry association had become the Automotive Transport Association of BC. *BC Trucking Association*

Most of the major haulers belonged to the Association, including Merchants Cartage, one of whose trucks is seen here transporting a boiler for BC Sugar Refinery Ltd. in 1948. City of Vancouver Archives CVA 1184-2193, Jack Lindsay photo

to form the General Cartage and Storage Association. The freighters had done well during the pre-war economic bustle and were looking to become an organized force able to make the case for the issues that concerned them: improved roads, fair rates, efficient regulation. As well, the suddenly deteriorating business climate must have made them hope that there was security in numbers. They were pioneers of a sort; it would be another thirteen years before the much more numerous Ontario trucking fraternity formed a similar organization.

In a sense the GCSA, the forerunner of today's BC Trucking Association, was a false start. Within a year the world was at war and the local freight business in disarray, along with just about everything else. Before long, essential war materials like rubber tires and gasoline were hard to come by, not to mention drivers, as young men flocked to join the armed forces. After five years though, peace brought a return to normality and during the 1920s the freight business grew apace, taking advantage of the new highways that had opened up in the Fraser Valley, south to the US border and then, in 1927, up the Fraser Canyon. The transition from horse power to horsepower was completed during this period, a change that was reflected at the end of the decade when the GCSA was reborn as the Commercial Motor Vehicle Owners' Association.

The Depression brought new challenges to the fledgling trucking industry, chiefly in the form of reduced business and increased competition. In 1934 the city of Vancouver introduced the first weight restrictions for commercial vehicles, and operators realized the increased importance of organization. In May of that year the short-lived CMVOA was replaced by a new organization, the Motor Carriers' Association (MCA). Led by some of the larger trucking companies in the province, the MCA addressed the problem of hyper-competition by lobbying the government to regulate the industry. The established companies chiefly wanted to make it harder for small operators, whose lower fixed costs enabled them to offer reduced freight rates, to enter the business. In response, the provincial government in 1940 established the Motor Carrier Branch, with a mandate to regulate licensing, tariffs and other

World War I threw the cartage business into disarray, not least of all because so many young drivers joined the armed forces. After the war, things returned to an even keel and the freight business began to expand rapidly. Here a group of soldiers arrives at Vancouver's Hastings Park with a load of hay in January 1919. When they demobilized, some of these young men may well have found work as drivers. City of Vancouver Archives CVA 99-761, Stuart Thomson photo

Above: A driver pays for his 1963 licence plate at the Licence Bureau Office in Vancouver.

Right: Note the number of different plates this vehicle had to display, a constant source of frustration for the industry.

Vancouver Public Library 41148; Courtesy of Wayne Ellis

matters. Headed by a superintendent of motor carriers, the branch carried out its activities under the auspices of the Public Utilities Commission. The creation of the MCB was the real beginning of economic regulation in the province and initially it was fully supported by the industry.

Meanwhile the Motor Carriers' Association was undergoing another reorganization. A number of the smaller operators had come to feel that the association was working mainly in the interests of the larger companies who wished to restrict the activities of the smaller outfits. In 1940 some of these dissidents broke away from the MCA to form their own lobbying organization, the Automotive Transport Association. By the end of the war the new association had grown to 187 member companies, while membership in the old MCA had fallen to fifty. But without a unified voice, neither association could speak effectively for the industry. Realizing this, the two sides settled their differences and in mid-1946 merged as the Automotive Transport Association of British Columbia. The ATABC would remain in existence for the next thirty-two years.

One issue that occupied the ATABC and its predecessor organizations for many years was the matter of municipal licence plates. The issue went all the way back to 1906, when the provincial government granted BC municipalities the power to issue licences and collect fees for commercial vehicles operating within their boundaries. This allowed municipalities to collect revenues to offset expenses related to the upkeep of local roads and it became an important source of local government revenue. At the same time, municipal licences were a major irritant for freight carriers who were asked to obtain a separate licence plate for each municipality in which they worked, a significant cost of doing business. As Harvie Malcolm, a former volunteer president of BCTA, recalled: "When I first got into the trucking side of the business [the 1940s], we had to have something like at least a dozen different licences, just to get as far as Hope. By the time you put the licence plates on the damn truck, you didn't have enough tare weight left to carry the load!" In 1957 one operator complained that he had to purchase twenty-eight licences just to work in the Lower Mainland alone.

The association lobbied long and hard for an end to the local plates, initially with little success. In 1964 H.M. Hartley, chair of the ATABC's municipal licensing committee, reported to the annual convention that the subject "has been on our agenda for so long that its mere mention makes some of us want to scream." However, Hartley had some good news to report. Four years earlier the provincial Royal Commission on Road User Charges agreed with the association that municipal licence fees were "excessive." The commission referred to the "jungle" of local levies on the trucking industry and called them "a barrier to inter-provincial commercial road transport." In 1963 the provincial government had responded to industry concerns by introducing a single municipal commercial vehicle licence plate that was valid throughout the province. The new system had to be worked out, and the size of the new fee scale negotiated, but Hartley was cautiously optimistic—though he warned industry representatives that the battle was not over. "We have to be realistic enough to realize that we don't stand a chance of getting away without municipal taxation," he told the convention. "All we can do is to fight to keep it within reasonable bounds." The new system mandated a single municipal licence plate (replaced by a decal in 1987), for each for-hire truck. It remains in place today, administered by the Union of BC Municipalities.

One of the services the ATABC offered its members was this annual directory.
Courtesy of Harvie Malcolm

Other postwar issues involving the ATABC included lobbying for improvements to the road network, the elimination of tolls on the Fraser Canyon Highway (they were removed in 1947), opposing preferential subsidies for the railways, the coordination of provincial licensing agreements to facilitate transnational freighting, and the gradual extension of load limits and vehicle size. In 1954, for example, when the city of Vancouver introduced its first trucking code to limit the size and weight of permissible loads and to establish truck routes through the city, the ATABC played a prominent part in the consultation process.

While association members agreed that progress was being made on these important economic matters, there was a sense that the ATABC was not yet as strong as it could be. In a 1962 report titled "Stability of the Motor Carrier Industry," the association's stability committee argued that owners of businesses were not as active in the ATABC as they should be and that as a result the group was lacking effective leadership. The alternative, the report pointed out, would be to hire a manager with a significant amount of authority. This alternative would not be accepted for another thirty years. In the meantime the result was an organization that was "very democratic" but less effective than it might be. Although the ATABC had about five hundred members at the time, the committee reported that meetings were badly attended and that many prominent carriers still did not belong, leaving the association unable to speak authoritatively for the industry.

By 1970 the stability committee's concerns had been addressed. As the decade began, the ATABC had grown to represent a significant proportion of the provincial industry. With growth came new

Commercial Plates

Motor Carrier Plates

The first licence plates issued by the provincial government for commercial vehicles appeared in 1924 with a T prefix (for Trucks). For some reason the plate was discontinued after one year and it was 1936 before the province began to issue annual licence plates for commercial vehicles, with a C prefix. The second plate down in the left column, one of the more eye-catching designs with the totem pole motif, was first issued in 1952 but was unfortunately scraped after eighteen months as the aluminum did not stand up to British Columbia's varied and harsh climate, and the renewal system was overly complicated and unwieldy. The third plate is a special issue to commemorate the province's centennial in 1958. Another interesting landmark: it was 1964 that the "Beautiful British Columbia" slogan was first used. In 1973 the letter prefix was dropped, but in 1976 letter suffixes were added. The current flag design began in 1985. In the right-hand column are special carrier plates indicating what each kind of truck was allowed to do. For example, in the top plate the K indicates a farm vehicle. The bottom plate shows a redesign, begun in 1988, that allowed plates to be revalidated with decals. *Courtesy of Ron Garay and Christopher Garrish*

Logging plates were not issued until 1961 (with a T prefix). They were issued quarterly, with the expiration date stamped at the top. Trailer plates first appeared in 1921. Starting in 1949 the T prefix was replaced by the word "trailer." In 1985 the flag was added, in common with other types of plates. The word, or abbreviation for, trailer was also removed, making it difficult to distinguish trailer plates from any others. Courtesy of Ron Garay and Christopher Garrish

challenges. The 1970s was a period of protracted labour difficulties, rising fuel costs, increasing irritation with government regulation and what was perceived to be unfair competition from the railways, particularly BC Rail. All of these issues, and others, kept the association busy. In 1978 members made a subtle shift in labelling when they agreed to change the name of their organization to the BC Motor Transport Association (BCMTA). The name change was in part an indication that the association intended to take a more active role in improving the public image of the industry. "Traditionally we've been a low profile industry," association president Harvie Malcolm told *BC Business* magazine. "We haven't believed in big lobbying efforts, basically feeling that the fundamental importance of our industry would speak for itself." It was time, Malcolm felt, to change the outdated public image of trucking by emphasizing how the industry had become a crucial contributor to the functioning of the modern economy.

Top: BCTA has sponsored an annual truck exposition, TRUXPO, every two years since the first took place in 1988. As of 2012 the event was taken over by a private trade show operator.

Below: Aficionados gather in 2011 at the annual show put on by the Vancouver Island Chapter of the American Truck Historical Society.

Courtesy of Black Knight Holdings, Randy & Donna Giesbrecht; Kevin Oke photo

The recession of the early 1980s hit the trucking industry hard. Revenues fell thirty-five percent as business contracted and fuel costs soared. The BCMTA responded to the "fuel crisis" and the imposition of successive government fuel tax increases by introducing its own fuel surcharge, the first of a series, in 1982. Customers weren't happy to pay higher rates, but for the most part they realized that the industry was responding to an unprecedented market situation over which it had no control.

In 1987 the association made its most recent name change, becoming the British Columbia Trucking Association. By that time it was deep into dealing with the impact of deregulation on the industry (the subject of the next chapter). Partly as a result of federal deregulation, the association was facing financial challenges and cast about for ways to generate revenue. George Lloyd of CP Bulk Systems, who was BCTA president at the time, asked Al Chorny of Freightliner of Canada to organize a truck show on behalf of the association. There had been a trade show during Expo 86 in Vancouver but it had been staged by a professional trade show company and had been overshadowed by the fair's other events. Nonetheless, Lloyd thought that a BCTA-organized event had the potential to be a money-maker. Under Chorny's chairmanship, a committee was formed to organize a biennial show and the name TRUXPO was chosen. The first TRUXPO took place at Canada Place on the Vancouver waterfront in 1988 and after three successful shows at that venue it moved in 1994 to the Trade and Exhibition Centre (TRADEX) in Abbotsford, where it has been held ever since. In 2011, deciding that TRUXPO had become so large and successful that it was imposing too much of a strain on association resources, BCTA sold the show to an independent trade show operator while remaining as sponsor and industry liaison.

Another important milestone for the association was the decision to hire a full-time president. For many years BCTA and its predecessors had been led by an executive secretary/general manager. Bill Morris held the job from 1957 to 1970, followed by Ray Hunt (1970–1986) and then Rob Weston

A vintage 1955 Mack B-61 owned by the Alberni Museum makes an appearance at the Vancouver Island truck show. Kevin Oke photo

Louise Yako took over behind the wheel as BCTA president in 2011. She succeeded Paul Landry, who had held the job since 1994.

Courtesy of Ken Johnson Trucking

(1986–1994). But the association's president had always been an industry professional who took on the job on a volunteer basis for a limited term. "Once [federal] deregulation came," George Lloyd explained, "the pressures on people in the industry were such that they didn't have the time to spend on association matters that they previously had." As well, members of the board came to feel that a full-time president, in the job for longer than a two-year term, would be a more effective spokesperson with government and help to improve the image of the industry with the general public. (The former president's position was retitled chairman and continues to be held on a two-year term by someone from the industry.) As a result, in the spring of 1994 Paul Landry, who had been working for Saskatchewan Government Insurance for several years, became the first full-time president of BCTA, a position he retained until he was succeeded by Louise Yako in 2011. With this structural change, the association became much more of a public-policy-oriented organization and its profile within the industry and with the provincial government increased dramatically. "The Ministry of Transportation and Infrastructure enjoys a highly positive relationship with the BCTA," says ministry COO Dave Byng. "We consider them one of our key sector stakeholders." As a result the association has been invited to work with government in a number of key policy areas, including highway safety, the harmonization of trucking regulations with other jurisdictions, the use of innovative truck-trailer configurations (such as LCVs), the impact of the industry on air quality and climate change generally, and many others.

During Landry's tenure BCTA was faced with a number of challenges that impacted a broad base of carriers in the province. One was vehicle safety, which emerged as a particular public concern following a series of troubling accidents in the 1990s. On July 9, 1990, a dump truck overloaded with hot asphalt rumbled into the ferry terminal parking lot at Horseshoe Bay and crashed into a recreational vehicle, killing a mother and her nine-year-old daughter. The driver of the truck, who was found to have

All motor vehicles, including trucks, used to be required to get regular inspections at government stations like this one on West Georgia near Stanley Park in Vancouver's West End in 1949. Nowadays, inspections aren't required for passenger vehicles, but commercial vehicles still undergo inspections every six months at government-licensed facilities. Vancouver Public Library 80876, Art Jones photo

cheated on his driving test, had failed to check his brakes; he was sentenced to three years in prison for criminal negligence. At the time the Horseshoe Bay crash seemed like a tragic but isolated incident, but it turned out to be a prelude to other serious accidents. On August 16, 1995, a truck-trailer travelling down the Cut, a steep hill on the Trans-Canada Highway in North Vancouver, lost its brakes and piled into several cars, killing the truck's driver, Baljinder Singh, and a driver in another car, Wayde Police. Subsequent investigations determined the truck had only about thirty percent of its braking capability. A year later an inquest jury looking into the incident made a series of recommendations to improve truck safety, including the hiring of more inspectors to monitor commercial vehicle safety; a toll-free phone number to report unsafe rigs; fines for drivers and owners with faulty brakes; roadside brake inspections; and new training programs for drivers. An ICBC specialist testified at the inquest that thirty percent of trucks on the road were not safe and news reports left the impression that uninspected trucks were a serious road hazard. As Paul Landry remarked about this period, "standing in front of a TV camera or a reporter's microphone defending the industry became a weekly, if not a daily, event." No sooner had the inquest reported than on September 5, 1996, a dump truck lost its brakes on a steep hill in Gibsons, north of Vancouver, and hurtled into the ocean, killing the driver and prompting the *Province* newspaper to urge the provincial government to take immediate action to "rid the trucking

Driver training offered by facilities like the Valley Driving School has become a critically important part of overall safety strategies by the industry. David Nunuk photo

industry of unsafe drivers and unscrupulous owners." Then, later in the month, as if to punctuate the *Province* editorial, another runaway dump truck with faulty brakes ran down a hill in West Vancouver and smashed into a car on Marine Drive, killing a fifty-eight-year-old pedestrian, Bjorn Bjornson, and injuring several other people. "Killer Trucks!" blared a headline on a story in *Reader's Digest* the following January.

Statistics indicated that the situation was not as dire as the public believed. In 1995 there were 4,727 heavy commercial vehicles involved in accidents in BC, which was just 4.7 percent of the fleet. Nonetheless, something had to be done and the provincial government responded to the public outcry by creating a joint government–industry task force to look into truck safety. The Task Force on Commercial Vehicle Safety (TFCVS) was co-chaired by Paul Landry and the superintendent of motor vehicles, Vicki Farrally. While it was deliberating, the provincial auditor general submitted a report on the Motor Vehicle Branch that was highly critical of its truck safety programs. This set the stage for the task force report, which appeared at the end of March 1997. The report made thirty-two recommendations, of which the government immediately implemented four, including higher fines for unadjusted brakes and a requirement that all operators of heavy trucks be able to take the written driver's test in English.

In spite of these efforts to improve truck safety, there continued to be a concern, both within the industry and among members of the public, that some companies were ignoring safety measures when it stood to benefit their bottom line—what Landry once called "the corner cutting practices of the bottom ten percent." One way BCTA chose to address this issue, along with the issue of attracting new drivers into the industry, was by advocating for higher standards for drivers and greater negative consequences for drivers and company owners who represented safety risks. The association encouraged improvements to the National Safety Code that would identify, and rid the industry of, negligent operators. As Landry told *Motor Truck* magazine in 2001, a small minority of under-qualified drivers were blackening the reputation of the industry as a whole. Part of the solution, he argued, was to make it more difficult

Professional drivers spend time in the classroom at the Mountain Transport Institute, a driving school in Castlegar.
Courtesy of Mountain Transport Institute Ltd.

to obtain a Class 1 licence so that drivers who do are more qualified and more conscious of their safety responsibilities. Raising the bar for new drivers, and for their employers, would improve the negative image of the industry, thought Landry, while also improving the public perception of the trucker.

At the same time, BCTA had been lobbying WorkSafeBC strenuously for funding to create a trucking safety council. Finally, in 2008, such a council was formed. The new BC Trucking Safety Council was intended to promote the development of a "culture of safety" within the industry in order to reduce the number of serious injuries and deaths. Another step in the same direction was taken in 2010 when the provincial government, in partnership with BCTA, launched a Premium Carrier Program to recognize companies that show a particular commitment to safety.

BCTA membership today consists of some of the largest carriers in the country, but most members are small to medium-sized operations, many of them family-owned. Almost seventy percent of member companies operate less than ten trucks; only six percent have more than fifty. In total, member companies operate about 18,000 vehicles with a wide variety of uses, including motor coaches, tankers, dump trucks, flat decks, reefers, moving vans, bulk haulers, highway tractor-trailers and more. As well, the association includes among its membership many supplier members, companies that provide goods

LeBlanc Trucking in Lumby was typical of the small trucking operations that have always characterized the BC industry. Note the licence plates displayed above the cab on this Pacific model logging truck, plus the tire chains decorating the front bumper.

Courtesy of Bob Dingsdale

These highway haulers are waiting their turn at a provincial weigh scale on Nordel Way in Delta. David Nunuk photo

and services to the trucking industry. The business of the association is guided by a six-person executive supported by a board of directors drawn from executives within the industry.

BCTA has a mandate to advance the interests of motor carriers in the province. It does so on many different fronts, including safety, infrastructure, labour issues, occupational health and safety, emissions regulations, weights and dimensions, port logistics and taxation, to name just a few. The border is another example. The association works on many initiatives with border agencies to expedite the passage of commercial vehicles between the US and Canada. Improvements have included the separation of commercial and automobile traffic, which began in the 1970s, the application of new technologies such as cargo x-ray and screening for radioactive materials, and the extension of hours of service. Prior to the year 2000, the Pacific Highway truck border crossing into the US was only open for LTL freight service from eight a.m. to ten p.m. five days a week and on Saturdays from eight a.m. to two p.m. On Sundays there was no LTL service at all, only single-bill trailer loads or empty trailers were allowed to cross. This was the fourth busiest commercial gateway between Canada and the US and, because of lack of staff, it was the only one of the four not open twenty-four hours a day, seven days a week. It was costing carriers a lot of money to hold shipments and accommodate waiting drivers, not to mention the time that was wasted. Finally, because of pressure from BCTA and the larger carriers, with assistance from the American Trucking Associations and greater understanding of the issue on the part of US customs officials, the Pacific border crossing in 2000 began processing trucks round the clock, seven days a week.

Within a year came the 9/11 attacks on New York City and Washington, DC, and increased security concerns at the border, which initially brought long delays. However, new programs and technologies were introduced that in many cases actually speeded up the processing of freight. Previously drivers heading south had arrived at the border with a trailer load of freight, then had to park on the Canadian side and walk all the paperwork related to each shipment to the offices of the various US customs

brokers for documentation entry. Drivers would wait for each broker to process the relevant paperwork, then walk back across the border and drive to customs to check in for entry processing. This was the first time that US customs officials were informed what was passing through and on the spot, with possibly a long line of trucks backed up at the crossing, they had to determine which shipments to examine and which to release for entry into the US. With the introduction of new information technologies and new processes, carriers began transmitting their paperwork electronically ahead of arrival. US customs officials now had a chance to pre-screen shipment documentation and to determine in advance of arrival which shipments required intensive examination. Drivers no longer had to make the cross-border walk to have their invoices and bills of lading entry documentation completed while they waited. Other programs expedited customs clearance for shippers and/or importers that had been pre-certified as not being a security risk. As a result, the border crossing became faster, as well as staying open to all carriers twenty-four hours a day. Still, border delays remain an issue for BC truckers and they welcomed the new agreement announced in December 2011 by Prime Minister Stephen Harper and US President Barack Obama aimed at harmonizing procedures on both sides of the border to speed up the crossing processes even further, in order to facilitate trade between the two countries.

Another major interest of BCTA is the "greening" of the fleet. Concerned that the general public sees the industry as environmentally unfriendly, the association emphasizes the many steps that manufacturers have taken to reduce harmful engine emissions and improve the fuel efficiency of the fleets. These include redesigning vehicle engines to activating speed limiters to the extensive use of new equipment to reduce vehicle drag, including side skirts, trailer fairings, low rolling resistance "super single" tires and auxiliary power units to reduce idling time. It is estimated that improved engine technology combined with "green" add-ons can reduce the greenhouse gas emissions produced by a single tractor-trailer by thirty percent. BCTA has lobbied extensively for provincial regulatory changes and financial incentives to improve the fuel efficiency of the fleet and it is cooperating with several local

The trucking industry has supported projects such as the Port Mann Bridge/ Highway 1 and South Fraser Perimeter Road projects, which are aimed at easing congestion and allowing goods to move more freely throughout the Lower Mainland.

David Nunuk photo

Shadow Lines, based in Langley, does more than carry freight. In 2010 the company converted this old shipping container into a portable homeless shelter providing warm, dry "rooms" for up to sixteen people on a winter night. Courtesy of Shadow Lines Transportation Group

and national organizations to investigate the practicality of any number of new technologies that might improve the industry's environmental performance.

In the Lower Mainland, the relationship between truckers and Port Metro Vancouver is an important issue. Since 2008 PMV has combined the operations of port facilities on Burrard Inlet, in the Fraser River and at Deltaport. It is the largest port in Canada and essential to its operation is the timely movement of containers to and from the docks. Trucks handle about thirty-five percent of this cargo so BCTA has an obvious interest in monitoring port policies that affect the transport of intermodal freight.

Another issue has been improvements to infrastructure—roads and bridges—around the province. One notable effort was to help convince the government to remove the tolls on the Coquihalla Highway, but this change was part of an ongoing consultation about highway financing in general. In the Lower Mainland, traffic congestion has been a growing problem. The vast majority of trucks operating in the province pass through this area so BCTA has a natural interest in trying to ensure that the traffic moves smoothly. The association has been an active supporter of the improvements to the Port Mann Bridge and the other road expansions that are part of the provincial government's Gateway Program. Beyond these infrastructure improvements, BCTA partners with a variety of industry and government agencies focussed on the challenges of ensuring that trade between North America and the Asia-Pacific region flows smoothly through BC, Canada's Pacific gateway.

As a member of the Canadian Trucking Alliance (CTA), the association is involved in a number of joint initiatives on behalf of the entire national industry. The alliance was formed in 1997 as a revitalized successor to the sixty-year-old Canadian Trucking Association. The new organization, which is a coalition of the seven provincial and regional trucking associations, brings the concerns of the industry to the attention of federal government officials on an ongoing basis. It also represents the trucking viewpoint in Washington, DC, on issues concerning border crossings, customs and trade. In addition to lobbying efforts at all levels of government, BCTA offers a variety of programs and services for its member companies. These include training and professional upgrading courses, scholarships, industry networking opportunities and a variety of affinity programs that direct members to reliable service providers.

Finally, one of the issues that informs all of the association's work is the public image of the industry. Trucking is a high-profile industry that relies on the good will of the public with whom it shares the highways. As such it has a vested interest in showing it understands and respects the values of the broader community. BCTA works to improve the public's estimation of the industry by addressing safety concerns, by emphasizing the important role trucking plays in the everyday life of British Columbians and by advocating with government in support of public policies that will enhance the ability of truckers to make their vital contribution to the economy of the province and the country.

Image Makeover

"The industry needs a lot of good public relations. When you say trucks to people on the street they think of the last one that cut them off, this kind of thing. I don't think the general public really perceives the critical nature of what trucks are to the economy. As we say, trucks deliver everything except babies."
— *George Lloyd*

Government and Trucking

Probably no development has had a greater impact on trucking in British Columbia than the economic deregulation of the industry that occurred beginning in the 1980s in the United States. In Canada, responsibility for regulating trucking is divided between the federal government, which regulates trucking between provinces, and the provincial governments, which regulate the industry within their jurisdictions. At the federal level, the government withdrew from regulation in 1988, while provincial economic regulation continued in BC until 1996, making this the last jurisdiction in

Governments have used tolls and taxes to pay for the highway system, going back to the Fraser Canyon Highway, which was a toll route when it opened in 1927. This photograph shows the construction of toll booths at the Pattullo Bridge shortly before it opened in November 1937.

Royal BC Museum, BC Archives E-01413

North America to deregulate. After that time governments continued to regulate safety issues and vehicle sizes and weights, but from a business perspective the industry today is wide open compared to what the situation was thirty years ago. The impact of deregulation was profound. Most people in the industry today say that the results were positive, though there are others who argue that the competitive environment it created may have led some operators to cut corners in areas such as safety and driver training, thereby contributing to a deterioration of the image of the driving profession in the eyes of the public.

An empty container truck leaves the docks at Port Metro Vancouver. The container side of the trucking industry is heavily regulated by government. David Nunuk photo

Following World War I, when trucking was in its infancy, it was an easy business to get into. The province's infrastructure, in the form of roads and bridges, was being built by the government at no expense to the trucker, aside from taxes, tolls and licence fees, which were minimal in those days. If someone wanted to start hauling furniture around town, or freight to the Interior, all they had to do was purchase a vehicle and find some customers. In 1925 the provincial government imposed the first regulations on the industry. According to an amendment to the Highway Act, a company involved in the commercial freight business needed to file a schedule of operations with the government and to obtain a "certificate of approval," later called a "certificate of public convenience and necessity." This was not an onerous requirement and still left the industry largely unregulated.

The Depression of the 1930s made the tendency toward hyper-competition in the industry even more marked as unemployed young men, desperate for work of any kind, scraped enough money together to buy used trucks and went into business for themselves. In hard times, they were willing to undercut their rivals and the result was a situation in which it was difficult for a company to build a

Under the regulations of the Motor Carrier Branch, trucking companies had to obtain licences to operate along specific routes in particular parts of the province. This map shows the different licence districts. BC Trucking Association

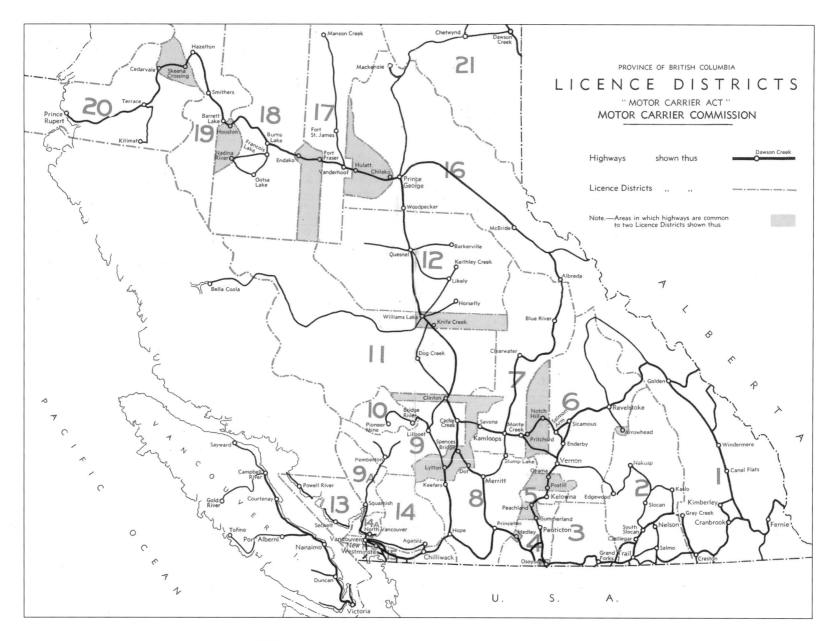

reliable customer base and invest in equipment; in other words, to grow. Increasingly, carriers that obtained the proper approvals were complaining that fly-by-night operators were stealing their business.

Unhappy with the instability, some industry leaders lobbied the provincial government, through the Motor Carriers' Association, the forerunner of BCTA, to address the issue of destructive competition. In 1940 the province enacted the Motor Carrier Act, which assigned regulation of the motor carrier industry to the Public Utilities Commission. The PUC in turn created the Motor Carrier Branch, with a superintendent of motor carriers, to bring some order to the industry by regulating who could enter the business. The government was willing to protect carriers from the effects of cutthroat competition. The public interest would not be served if a race to the bottom lowered revenues so far that no carrier could remain in business. At the same time the government wished to ensure that every community in the province received adequate freight service. It also recognized that the physical geography of the province, with its steep grades and narrow thoroughfares, made it necessary to control the use of the road system.

Under regulations devised by the PUC and elaborated on over the next fifty years, carrier companies applied to the commission for operating licences, also known as authorities. These licences of carriage (as distinct from vehicle licences) authorized a company to operate along specific routes in particular areas of the province. As time went on they became ever more specific, imposing a variety of other restrictions—from the type of freight that was carried to the shipping schedule and the size of a company's fleet. Sometimes licences were granted for specialized cartage; for example, explosives, or "heavy loads" (heavy machinery or lumber), or for "charter trips," in which the driver and truck were under contract to a shipper to transport specific goods (such as milk for the Fraser Valley Milk Producers or minerals from a particular mine). The commission also required companies to file their rates and to submit and justify any changes to these rates. Initially the operations of the Motor Carrier Branch were handled by a single superintendent of motor carriers based in Vancouver. In 1973 the new NDP government abolished the Public Utilities Commission and amended the Motor Carrier Act to create a three-person Motor Carrier Commission to regulate the industry under the authority of the ministry of transportation.

For many years carriers supported economic regulation. At the end of 1961, the industry association, then the ATABC, appointed a "stability committee" to study issues related to the perceived "unstable conditions and general lack of prosperity" in the industry. In its report the committee, chaired by S. Keith Jackson of T & H Cariboo Transport and later Public Freightways, emphasized that "the economic geography of the province of British Columbia demands a planned and controlled motor transport system." The report argued that the concentration of population in the Lower Mainland, combined with a sparsely populated hinterland, meant that the government needed to control entry to the industry while ensuring that communities in the Interior received regular service. "The absence of restrictive licensing would undoubtedly lead to uneconomical operations and overloading of limited road resources." Indeed, the committee pointed out a number of ways that the Motor Carrier Branch should extend its reach—for example, to police farmers who were working from time to time as for-hire haulers and to regulate contract carriers who were expanding their operations beyond their original contract into areas for which they were not licensed. To the degree that the stabilization committee spoke for the entire industry, BC truckers seemed to want more regulation, not less. In 1965 ATABC executive secretary Bill Morris urged the government to limit the entry of new carriers into what he described as an already crowded marketplace. "As rates are slashed, so are margins," he said. "The corporate corpses pile up, and everyone suffers."

A company applying to obtain an operating authority to serve a particular licence district (no licences were granted for the province as a whole) had to convince the commission first of all that

A couple of big rigs, a Kenworth on the left and a Hayes on the right, wait at the Kingsgate border crossing into Idaho. Note the number of licence plates that each vehicle had to display. The cumulative cost of licence fees was an ongoing grievance with truckers.
Courtesy of Kevin Duddy

A Cypress Transfer moving van negotiates the streets of Vancouver in 1971. Cypress eventually belonged to the Johnston Terminals constellation of companies. Courtesy of Dietmar Krause

A Merchant's Cartage flatbed manoeuvres the fuselage of a Grunman Goose through the intersection at Granville and Broadway in Vancouver in the 1940s. By this time civic governments had adopted the idea of designated truck routes through urban areas and the company would need to get special permission to haul such an oversized load through city streets. Courtesy of Dietmar Krause

existing service to that district was inadequate, and secondly that the applicant was able to improve on it. It did this by marshalling support from customers who would back the application. Naturally enough, a carrier who was already serving a destination would often oppose any application from a competitor. The result was a costly, time-consuming, often acrimonious, process of public hearings. "This was a whole industry that was created for the legal profession," recalled Dietmar Krause, who got his start at Johnston Terminals.

The expectation was that in return for adhering to the detailed conditions of its licence, a carrier would receive protection from competition, at least along a particular route. "It made it difficult to enter the industry," explained George Lloyd, "and once you were in you were very insulated from economic reality." Other areas of regulation involved load weights and vehicle measurements, hours that drivers were permitted to be behind the wheel and safety measures. While the industry consulted with the government about them, these procedural regulations were far less contentious than the licensing procedures.

Because it was so difficult to obtain an operating authority by approaching the Public Utilities Commission (and later the Motor Carrier Commission), companies wanting to expand their service into a particular district preferred to do so by purchasing a competing carrier that already had the appropriate licence. In this way some large carriers extended their reach to Vancouver Island and across the Interior. During the 1960s, for example, Johnston Terminals expanded in this way. "In transportation, the main thing you need is an operating authority, a licence for a route," explained the president of Johnston at the time, Ron Granholm, to *BC Business* magazine. "These aren't readily available, and to get them is a long process. If you're lucky, you can apply for them through a regulatory authority, but they're not always available, so the only way you can get them is by acquisition. That's one of the reasons why, quite often, you have to acquire companies to expand into an area where you are not presently serving." Johnston purchased a number of companies during this period: Public Freightways, Pacific Terminals in North Vancouver, Inland Tanker Services of Port Moody, heavy-haul specialist Merchant Cartage, Heaney Cartage in Victoria, West Coast Freight in Nanaimo, Shorty's Transport in Edmonton and others. Several prominent outfits followed the same strategy, though not many to the same extent as Johnston.

John Bourbonniere tells an interesting story about how Yellow Transportation obtained operating authority in BC. Yellow was a US-based transcontinental general freight carrier operating a hub and spoke network of over 350 terminals in the US and operations in Quebec. Due to the regulated environment it was all but impossible to secure an operating authority by applying to the MCC, and Yellow was using interline carriers from Seattle with operating rights in BC to finalize BC deliveries on goods from the US. But Yellow had its eye on obtaining an authority to haul directly into the province. One day in 1984 Tony Toews, a sales representative for Yellow, was leafing through the operating authorities that the various companies had. (These were a matter of public record and available for viewing at the MCC offices.) Toews noticed that a small Lower Mainland courier company, Custom Courier, actually had a full general freight authority with an unrestricted licence to haul freight in and out of the Lower Mainland. The owner, John Milne, did not have any interest in being a full freight operation. Seeing the opportunity, Yellow made an offer to purchase Custom Courier, which would give Yellow the entry into the province that it desired. Initially the MCC refused to approve the purchase, saying there must have been a mistake in the original paperwork. Yellow stuck to its guns, arguing that the licence was unrestricted, whether it was intended at the time of original issue or not. In the end the MCC had no option, the sale was approved and very quickly Yellow became a major cross-border carrier serving BC.

The difficulty of obtaining operating authorities was just one aspect of government regulation that the industry began to feel frustrated about. As time passed, the inefficiencies associated with the MCC

This is a Kenworth half-shack belonging to Yellow Transit, later Yellow Transportation, an American carrier which had trouble getting authority to operate in BC.

Right and opposite: Every summer Duncan hosts an Antique Truck Show, put on by the Vancouver Island chapter of the American Truck Historical Society. Among the vehicles on display in 2011 were this 1953 International Harvester, owned by Curtis Frueh of Duncan, and (next page) a 1951 Mack A-40H with its shiny bulldog hood ornament, owned by Tony Splane of Sedro-Wooley, Washington State, and a 1946 Fargo three-ton Special owned by Morris Dougan of Cobble Hill. Kevin Oke photos

became increasingly time-consuming and illogical. "Some of the silliness was," explained Dietmar Krause, "if you were going from Vancouver to Prince George and that's what your licence said, you couldn't stop in Williams Lake or Quesnel, even though you drove through it every day." Likewise a carrier licensed to haul a particular product to a destination might not have any authority to carry a return load of something else. This situation resulted in a lot of interlining. Carriers without a licence to operate in a certain area would interline freight to a carrier that did. The result was delivery delays and increased tariffs.

Combined with these issues was the problem of enforcement, or lack of enforcement. Rhys Evans, who worked for the largest courier company in the province during the 1980s and later wrote an academic thesis about the industry, explains that competitors often violated the regulations by carrying loads for which they were not licensed, serving destinations that were not part of their authority and charging less than they were supposed to. When Evans's company complained to the MCC, it was told that the commission simply did not have the staff to police its own regulations. Similarly, Harvie Malcolm of Johnston Terminals explains that sometimes an operator would apply for a courier, or small parcel, licence, then gradually increase the size of these "parcels" until the operator was offering what was in essence an unlicensed full freight service. Yet the MCC, when asked to intervene, claimed it was

Another visitor to the Antique Truck Show was this gleaming 1979 International Harvester COE Transtar, owned by Fred Williston in Sidney. Kevin Oke photo

too busy. Without effective enforcement, honest carriers were punished for playing by the rules while unscrupulous carriers stole their business. For all these reasons, by the 1980s opinion within the industry was beginning to shift against regulation, at least as it was working in BC.

Legal Here, Illegal There

"In addition to the operating regulations, there was another set of regulations that dealt with the weight and dimensions of your equipment. And that too could be very onerous. Some of these politicians, just to be difficult and not to agree with anybody on their borders, would make things different, for no logical reason. Alberta and BC would be that way. It made it very difficult for anyone operating, trying to haul freight across the country. What was legal here was illegal there, and so on."
— *George Lloyd*

In the United States economic deregulation of interstate trucking began in the early 1980s. The Canadian government followed suit in 1987 with passage of the Motor Vehicle Transport Act, leading to the deregulation of interprovincial trucking early the following year. There was a general trend at this time for governments to get out of the transportation sector, despite having played such an important role in it historically. In Canada, Ottawa privatized Canadian National, the publicly owned railway, in 1995, handed management of the airports to independent, not-for-profit authorities and reorganized the ports. The deregulation of trucking took place in this new ideological context. The intention was to reduce impediments to interprovincial trade and to make it easier for companies to enter the industry, thereby increasing competition and allowing market forces to make carriers more efficient.

At the same time as federal deregulation was taking effect the industry was experiencing the impact of the free trade agreement with the United States. The idea of a formal pact had been proposed by a 1985 Royal Commission on Canada's economic prospects and the Conservative government of Brian Mulroney decided to make it a reality. In the autumn of 1988 the Conservatives won a hard-fought election over the issue and the Canada–United States Free Trade Agreement took effect on January 1, 1989. (It was expanded to include Mexico under the North America Free Trade Agreement in 1994.) Because about seventy percent of all Canada–US trade travels by truck, when the FTA (and later NAFTA) increased trade significantly between the participating countries it had obvious ramifications for Canadian carriers. While increased competition from American-owned companies led to the closure and consolidation of a significant number of Canadian firms, the FTA also brought about an increase in the level of cross-border traffic for Canadian truckers. According to a study done for Statistics Canada, north-south shipments in both directions increased by eight percent a year during the early 1990s. To take just one example of what this meant in practical terms, John Bourbonniere calculated that before free trade, for every five trailers his company, Yellow Transportation, brought north into Canada, four returned to Seattle empty; following the agreement he estimated that only two out of five trailers were going back empty, which amounted to a significant increase in revenue.

If the early 1990s brought increased volumes for cross-border carriers, the domestic industry was not in such good shape. With deregulation, existing carriers were encouraged to meet increased competition by keeping their rates low. The same Statistics Canada study showed that from 1989 to 1991 the industry downsized in order to compensate for lower rates. The number of bankruptcies among

Aside from economic regulation, governments have always had a role in regulating vehicle weights and lengths. One of the reasons that the cab-over-engine (COE) design was popular was that it reduced the length of the cab and allowed more room for freight. This is a Carson Truck Lines tractor-trailer rig at Williams Lake in 1969. Courtesy of Bruce Harger

carrier companies in Canada peaked in 1991 at 763, and profitability continued to be low during the whole period. At the same time, because companies were forced to become leaner and more competitive they also became more efficient. Nationwide, the industry emerged from this difficult period, in the words of the StatsCan study, "better managed and more productive."

Meanwhile, in BC the trucking industry continued to be irritated by regulation. Most other provinces followed the lead of the federal government and loosened their grip on the industry but BC was slow to fall into step. Indeed, BC was the last jurisdiction in North America to have government still involved in the business of trucking, with the MCC still enforcing the system of operating authorities. Paul Landry recalled that when he became president of BCTA in 1994 he was surprised at the control

A Canadian Freightways A-train hauls through the Fraser Valley. When economic deregulation arrived in the 1990s it was a challenge for the industry. The companies that found ways to adapt survived; those that for one reason or another could not, did not.

David Nunuk photo

that the provincial government still had on the industry. "When I got here," said Landry, "the biggest single frustration was the Motor Carrier Commission of the day that was involved in every aspect of trucking. We said, 'you don't regulate drycleaners, you don't regulate restaurants.' These businesses decide whether or not they want to enter the business or leave the business or grow the business based on the economics of the industry. The government should be concerned about whether there are cockroaches in the restaurant or E. coli in the vegetables, but that is a different kettle of fish from economic regulation. There was no case whatsoever for the government to be managing the affairs of trucking companies."

Discussions to improve the situation continued. The government was not unsympathetic to the frustrations of the industry but it had concerns of its own. If deregulation occurred, what would be the impact on the less densely populated areas of the province, where freight service was not always profitable? Would adequate service continue? Would vehicle safety standards be maintained? Would there be a sudden shift away from high-paying unionized jobs to non-unionized labour? Would a deregulated industry result in regional disparity? Would large carriers prosper at the expense of smaller companies? These were all legitimate concerns, but the proponents of deregulation felt that they could be addressed while at the same time resolving the inefficiencies of the current system of licensing authorities. Support for change was not unanimous in the industry, however. Some companies were happy with the prevailing system, which was working to their advantage. But most everyone was frustrated at the time and expense it took for the MCC to make its decisions related to operating authorities and permit applications. BCTA officially backed deregulation for a variety of reasons. It argued that the current system was inefficient; that it presumed that the government could manage the affairs of trucking companies better than the companies themselves; that it involved a lot of bureaucratic time wasting; that it stifled innovation and customer service; and that deregulation was a continent-wide phenomenon against which BC could not logically be the only holdout. Finally, BCTA pointed out, the regulations were not being enforced fairly anyway.

In the end it was the federal government that again forced everyone's hand. In June 1996 Bill C-88 received royal assent. This bill, when it was proclaimed at the beginning of 1998, would remove from the provinces the authority to regulate the hauling of freight within any particular province by carriers who also operated outside that province. A province could continue to regulate intra-provincial carriers but obviously this would put them at a competitive disadvantage compared to extra-provincial carriers, which would be unregulated. As a result, in the fall of 1996 it seemed as if the time had come to transform the regulatory regime in BC.

Admitting as much, the provincial government replaced the head of the Motor Carrier Commission, whose relationship with the trucking industry had become acrimonious. Then the minister of transportation appointed a panel of MLAs to review the status of motor carrier regulation. The panel heard many complaints about the inefficiencies of the MCC and on May 1, 1997, it released a report slamming the commission for being insensitive to the needs of the industry it was supposed to be regulating and recommending almost full deregulation.

On January 1, 1998, complete economic deregulation arrived in BC. The MCC was not abolished but its role was changed. The system of operating authorities was abandoned. Any carrier could compete for business on any route at any price. The government still kept a close watch on safety issues and vehicle sizes, but as far as the terms of doing business, it was now an open market. Although it had been called for by the industry, deregulation brought profound disruption. "I suggest that the entire industry was overwhelmed by it," said Harvie Malcolm. "It shook the industry to the core," agreed George Lloyd. In the deregulated market, carriers competed for business by lowering rates. Established companies, some with unionized workforces, faced competition from new carriers without the large infrastructure and union contracts to support. There was a feeling that some outfits tried to meet lower rates by saving on vehicle safety and driver training. "To the degree that there is unfair competition, and there is," argued Paul Landry, "it is because some carriers are cutting corners." To exacerbate the situation, there had been a downturn in the Canadian economy during the early 1990s so companies were already feeling the pinch.

Some companies survived deregulation and did very well. Others did not. An example of a company that did not was Sidney Freight Ltd. on Vancouver Island. Founded in 1952 by Norm Jackson and his wife, Marg, as J & J Transfer and Storage, a furniture moving business in Victoria, the company grew in the conventional way by purchasing other Island operators and their operating licences. One of the businesses purchased was Sidney Freight Service, which was acquired in 1964 and traced its origins back to 1920. In 1980 the freight divisions of the company amalgamated to create Sidney Freight Ltd., by then managed by Norm's son Gerry Jackson. The company also owned three moving companies, a maintenance division, a Campbell River–based operation serving the north Island called Haida Transport and a freight service in the Gulf Islands. The combined operation consisted of sixty power units and seventy trailers and operated into Vancouver as well as along the Island routes. But in January 1995 the *Times Colonist* newspaper in Victoria informed its readers that the "Island's biggest Truck firm" was going out of business. The reasons why a company fails are usually varied but certainly one of the

Opposite: Roadside weigh stations are one way the government regulates highway truck traffic. There are twenty-three scales across BC. This one is at the Pacific Highway truck border crossing in Surrey. David Nunuk photo

factors in the case of Sidney Freight was the highly competitive business climate that accompanied the deregulation of the trucking industry. Of course Sidney Freight was not alone. All across the province mergers and closures occurred as those in the industry struggled to come to terms with the new situation.

With the arrival of deregulation there was an increased emphasis on customer service and the streamlining of delivery systems. In such a competitive environment, companies had to become more responsive to the needs of shippers. Improved inventory management, just-in-time delivery and track and trace technologies all became weapons in the arsenal of trucking companies seeking to retain their customers. At the same time operators also looked to the application of new engine technologies that would help the bottom line.

Of course, the new regime did not mean the end of all government regulations. One niggling issue that remained was the requirement for motor carrier plates. Before deregulation, these were used to limit the fleet size of for-hire carriers. All vehicles were required to have an annual plate at a cost of one hundred dollars. The MCC collected about $6 million a year from these plates. Once deregulation was introduced, the industry lobbied to have them abolished, arguing that since there was no longer a regulatory system there was no need to keep charging fees to pay for it. Finally, in 1998, motor carrier plates were abolished.

Beyond that, both federal and provincial governments retained the authority to regulate certain non-business aspects of the industry. If the market was now open to anyone who wanted to enter, government and industry were concerned that safety standards could be thrown to the wind, so in 1987 a National Safety Code was introduced to set safety standards to which the industry had to adhere. Government still controls truck weights and dimensions because of their impact on the condition of the public highways and on safety. Environment Canada sets emissions standards. Federal, provincial and local governments all impose fuel taxes. There are regulations related to the transport of dangerous goods, and municipalities control truck routes and enforce noise bylaws. Trucking is not a regulation-free enterprise by any means. But compared to the straitjacket of rules and procedures that bound the industry in its formative stages, carriers now function in a competitive marketplace free from the interference of government economic regulators.

The Industry Looks Ahead

During its first century of service to the local and national economy, BC's trucking industry has overcome a series of daunting challenges to its success. First and foremost was the difficult geography of the province. BC is not an easy place to access and the variety of its terrain makes it the most challenging place in North America to operate a truck. From the east the way is blocked by the barrier of the Rockies, backed up by a series of lesser but still formidable mountain chains. From the coast, travellers must wind their way up narrow river valleys and climb through high alpine passes.

Impressive as it is to look at, this chrome and steel monster with its flat nose and belching smokestacks belongs to another era. Today the industry puts a premium on leaner, and greener. David Nunuk photo

Just think back to January 9, 1965, when many tons of earth, snow and stone rumbled down the sides of a mountain ridge east of Hope and covered a three-kilometre (almost two-mile) stretch of the Hope–Princeton Highway under 70 metres (230 feet) of debris. Three vehicles were buried in the muck, including a tanker truck and its driver. Searchers never recovered the bodies of two of the four people who died. No question it was the worst rock slide in BC history, but in fact slides, of both snow and rock, are among the most common geological hazards in the province. They remind us just how difficult and dangerous negotiating the mountainous interior of BC can be. It is a terrain that challenged the nerves of the early truckers, and even with all the improvements to their vehicles over the years, it still does.

If geography was the first challenge the pioneer truckers overcame, the limits of technology was the second. In those early trucks with their puny engines and faulty brakes, you had to be a bit of the daredevil to get behind the wheel of one of them. It was an *uncomfortable* job, as well as a dangerous one. Of course, that changed over the years as mechanics and engineers got to work designing the high-powered engines, driver-friendly cabs and streamlined rigs that are part of the industry today.

The next challenge was presented by the economics of trucking. It was from the beginning a highly competitive business with few barriers to anyone who wanted to get involved. Combined with the constantly rising costs of doing business, particularly labour costs and, at least since the 1970s, the steadily rising price of fuel, this meant that companies had to be light on their feet when it came to finding innovative ways to meet the bottom line, and more service oriented to keep their customers satisfied.

Trucking is a public service as well as a private enterprise. People rely on the products that trucks deliver. Recognizing this, government began regulating the industry early on to ensure that carriers visited all parts of the province. Of course, the sometimes capricious regulations imposed by the government were yet another challenge that carriers had to accommodate. With the economic deregulation of the industry in the 1990s, relations with the government became less adversarial and the industry now

Above: Even as it moves forward, the industry recalls its past, symbolized here by a 1949 Diamond T, owned by the BC Forest Discovery Centre in Duncan, and on show in Duncan at the Antique Truck Show held by the Vancouver Island chapter of the American Truck Historical Society. Kevin Oke photo

Left: The industry is always looking to improve safety standards and one way is to enhance driver training. David Nunuk photo

Opposite: BC's sinuous mountain ranges and steep river valleys make it one of the most difficult terrains in North America for trucking. David Nunuk photo

Another reminder of the past is this 1942 Dodge Logger (above and right) owned by the Rankin family and photographed at a recent vintage truck show. Kevin Oke photos

works cooperatively with the province in the development of a wide range of transportation policies. And most recently, truckers have had to meet the green imperative, the need to shed their image as smoke-belching, gas-guzzling polluters, and become leaner and cleaner in their operations.

So much for the past. What are some of the challenges facing motor carriers as they haul ahead into the future? One is the border. Delays at the border crossings resulting from security concerns are costing carriers time, and time means money. Since 9/11 various procedures have been introduced in co-operation with US Customs and Border Protection to speed the processing of freight, and carriers are hoping that this trend continues. Another challenge is presented by the driver shortage. The industry

As long as loggers are cutting down trees, truckers will be moving them to the mill, just one of the ways the industry is essential to the provincial economy. David Nunuk photo

has faced a shortage of qualified drivers for several years. A large number of drivers are reaching retirement age at the same time as young people, men and women, are reluctant to make a career of trucking, whether because the lifestyle does not suit them or because they have a negative impression of what driving entails. In BC the industry has responded with programs to improve driver training. Driving truck may never enjoy the cachet it once did, when drivers were admired and respected as "knights of the road," but there is no reason why it cannot appeal to anyone who is looking for a satisfying career that is well paid, flexible, challenging and service oriented.

The greening of the fleet that has been going on for several decades will continue to preoccupy carriers in the future. The industry has responded to the requirements of stricter emissions standards by converting to low-sulphur fuel and utilizing cleaner equipment. Reducing fuel consumption became a top priority, as was reflected in the adoption of aerodynamic styling and improved driving practices. Vehicles today may resemble their counterparts from thirty years ago, but they are as dissimilar as a Mercedes is from a Model T. Modern trucks utilize a variety of technological advances, from low rolling resistance tires to computerized monitoring of almost every aspect of their operation. Some even fill their tanks with alternative fuels to the ultra-low-sulphur diesel that is now the industry standard. All these innovations are aimed at reducing the impact the vehicles have on the environment. Not every truck has made the transition, but the industry as a whole is moving in the green direction.

As BC expands its role as the gateway to the Asia-Pacific region, the trucking industry will continue to play its crucial role in the movement of goods. David Nunuk photo

To the public, trucks may seem intimidating, even dangerous. Size matters. The larger the vehicles become, the more they seem to loom ominously over the motorists who share the roads with them. As it moves into the future the industry will need to convey to the public the progress it is making in the areas of safety, service and sustainability. In other words, it has to work on its image.

But perhaps the greatest challenge facing the industry is the challenge of growth. As BC's economy expands, fuelled in large part by the expansion of trade with the Asia-Pacific region, the need for improved transportation, and in particular more trucks, will increase. Growth will require enhanced infrastructure—roads, bridges, ports, railways—to keep the supply line flowing smoothly. As a crucial part of the distribution network, trucks are going to become more necessary, and more plentiful. The challenge will be to manage growth so as to deal with the issues of labour supply, population density and traffic congestion, which are all its inevitable side effects.

Trucking is vital to British Columbians. Without trucks to transport natural resources, consumer goods and manufacturing inputs, the economy would cease to function. That is the job BC's motor carrier industry has been performing since the first horseless carriage appeared in the streets about a hundred years ago. Can it be accomplished more cleanly, more safely and more efficiently? Absolutely.

That is the challenge of the second century of trucking in British Columbia.

ACKNOWLEDGEMENTS AND SOURCES

I'd like to thank the many people involved in different aspects of the trucking industry in BC who helped bring this project to fruition. Louise Yako, and her predecessor as president and CEO of the BC Trucking Association, Paul Landry, were both extremely forthcoming with information and oversight. Shelley McGuinness coordinated the project for BCTA, putting me in touch with sources of information and organizing my access to the records that the association has in its possession. Also at BCTA, thanks to the people who read an early version of the manuscript and made many useful suggestions to improve it: Trace Acres, John Bourbonniere, Greg Kolesniak, Jim White and Greg Munden. Jack Vleeming, a driver for Clark Freightways, accepted me into his cab and put up with my insistent questions about the driving life as we travelled through the night together to Prince George. Thanks to Greg Rogge and Marcus Clark at Clark Freightways for making that trip possible. As well as granting me an interview, Harvie Malcolm allowed me access to his collection of documents relating to the history of Johnston Terminals, BCTA and the trucking industry generally. Harvie was an enthusiastic proponent of the book project from the beginning and it would have been difficult to complete without his support. Jay Brandt, formerly the assistant port director for trade operations with US Customs and Border Protection, provided useful information about the border crossings. Ted Campbell shared his compilation of stories gathered during fifty years as a driver. Sabik Singh shared documents relating to his family's history and to his own involvement as an activist in the industry. John Wihksne, a member of a pioneering BC trucking family, was generous with his first-hand knowledge of driving and his own research into the history of the industry. I am grateful to the many people who contributed photographs to the project. These include: Christopher Garrish and Ron Garay who provided the license plates (anyone interested in this aspect of the subject should check out Chris Garrish's website www.BCpl8s.ca); Greg Rogge, Clark Freightways; Don Tamaki, Campion Boats; Alycia Majorkiewicz-Ata, Port Metro Vancouver; Zach Williams, Williams Moving and Storage; Louisa Genzale, Northern Sentinel Press, Kitimat; Rod Neufeld, Argus Carriers; Hank Suderman, www.hankstruckpictures.com; R.B. Skillings and Cathy Kellett, Victoria Van and Storage; Andy Roberts, Mountain Transport Institute, Castlegar; Shelley Harding, Alberni Valley Museum; Alisha Rubadeau, The Exploration Place, Prince George; Liz Ellison, Greater Vernon Museum and Archives; Florence Smith, Northern BC Archives & Special Collections, University of Northern BC, Prince George; Jennifer Yuhasz, Jewish Museum and Archives of BC, Vancouver; Leslie Middleton and Elizabeth Hunter, Quesnel & District Museum and Archives; Adrian Mitescu, Pacific Newspaper Group; Louise Avery, Kitimat Museum & Archives; Toula Marra, Museum Victoria (Australia); Sandra Parrish, Museum at Campbell River; Kelly-Ann Turkington, BC Archives, Victoria; City of Vancouver Archives; Special Collections, Vancouver Public Library; Sarah Romkey, UBC Special Collections; Kathryn Gagnon, Cowichan Valley Museum and Archives, Duncan; Lorna Dishkin, BC Central Coast Archives, Bella Coola; Jeannette Lorenz, Valemount Museum and Archives; Derryll White, Columbia Basin Institute of Regional History, Cranbrook; Donna Johnson, Kelowna Public Archives; Heather Stephens, Vanderhoof Community Museum; John Wihksne; Bruce Harger; Dave McIntosh; Gordon Hay; Jan Clemson; Rod Parkinson; Mark Simiele; Gary McLeod; Wayne Ellis; Dale Nelson; Brad Reddecopp; Kevin Duddy; Bruce Shantz; Hank Rabe; Gerri Logan; Bob Dingsdale; Dennis Bowcott; Tony Gussie; Trudy Jarvis; Vic Goertzen; Don Querciagrossa; Bob Gammer; and Mike Boissonneault. Thanks to Kevin Oke for documenting the American Truck Historical Society Antique Truck Show in Duncan, as well as to all the truck owners who participated and graciously allowed their rigs to be photographed. My appreciation to David Nunuk who spent months travelling the highways of British Columbia in order to visually document contemporary trucking in BC (and who even broke his finger scrambling up a cliff in order to getting just the right shot in Lytton). Stephen Ullstrom, production assistant at Harbour Publishing, deserves special mention for coordinating the collection of these many images. And finally, thanks to the people listed below who agreed to be interviewed about their experiences in the industry.

Interviews

Dick Bandstra, retired, Bandstra Transportation Systems Ltd.

John Bandstra Sr., retired co-founder, Bandstra Transportation Systems Ltd.

Shub Bawa, Marpole Transport Ltd.

John Berryere, retired driver

John Bourbonniere, retired, YRC Reimer (formerly Yellow Transportation)

Dave Byng, COO, Ministry of Transportation and Infrastructure; president and CEO, BC Rail Company

Marcus Clark, president, Clark Freightways

Ray Cotton, general manager, Inland Kenworth

Ingrid Giesbrecht, driver, Ken Johnson Trucking Ltd.

Bob Green, retired driver

Bruce Harger, retired driver

Joyce Hendriks, retired CEO, Clark Freightways

Angela Jones, driver, Ken Johnson Trucking Ltd.

Dietmar Krause, TMS Transportation Management Services Ltd.

Paul Landry, former BCTA president and CEO, 1994–2011

Shirls Leclerc, driver, Berry & Smith Trucking Ltd.

Frank Linke, retired trailer mechanic

George Lloyd, retired, Trimac Bulk Systems

Norm Lynch, Teamsters Freight Transportation Museum and Archives

Harvie Malcolm, retired, Johnston Terminals

Gregg Rogge, vice-president and general manager, Clark Freightways

Fergus Savage, transportation safety consultant

Bruce Shantz, retired driver

Mal Shephard, retired, Detroit Diesel

Sabik Singh, retired owner, G.H. Singh and Sons Trucking

Tony Toews, retired senior account executive, Yellow Transportation Inc.

Jake Wall, retired driver

Hans Wettstein, driver, Canadian Freightways

Frank White, retired driver

Jim White, general manager, Commercial Logistics Inc.

John Wihksne, retired driver

Neil Woolliams, former President of West Rim Express Lines

Magazines

BC Business
BCTA Herald
Motor Carrier (March 1968–January 1972)
Today's Trucking
Truck-N-West (December 1975–May 1977)

Acknowledgements and Sources

Websites and Articles Consulted Online

Garrish, Christopher John. "British Columbia Commercial Truck License Plates," at www.bcpl8s.ca/Commercial-Truck.html, consulted August 19, 2011.

———. "British Columbia Motor Carrier License Plates," at www.bcpl8s.ca/MotorCarrier.htm, consulted August 19, 2011.

———. "British Columbia Municipal License Plates," at www.bcpl8s.ca/Municipal.htm, consulted August 19, 2011.

Ministry of Transportation and Highways. *Frontier to Freeway: A Short Illustrated History of the Roads in British Columbia*. Victoria: Government of BC, undated (accessed online at www.th.gov.bc.ca/publications/frontiertofreeway/index.htm).

Rabe, H. "Pacific Truck and Trailer History," at www.pacifictruckclub.org/history.php, consulted November 1, 2011.

Virtual Museum of Canada. "Early Truckers: The History of Trucking in Canada," at www.virtualmuseum.ca/Exhibitions/Highway/en/index.html, consulted March 14, 2011.

Wilson, Ian. "CNR Trucking: Express and Freight Vehicles," at www.images.technomuses.ca/?en/stories/freight-vehicles/intro/page/1, consulted March 14, 2011.

Unpublished Sources

Automotive Transport Association of BC. "Stability of the Motor Carrier Industry," the report of the ATABC's Committee of Investigation, 1962.

BC Trucking Association. Scrapbooks of newspaper articles, 1995–2011.

Campbell, Ted. "Trucker Tales: Fifty Years of Trucking, from Flathead Ford to Long Nose Pete," typescript courtesy of the author.

Johnston Group. "The Johnston Group, Corporate History," a transcript of an interview with Harvie Malcolm.

Kolesniak, Greg. "Establishment and Vehicle Statistics," a report prepared for the BC Trucking Association, August 2008.

Royal Commission on Road User Charges. "Report of the 1960 Commission of Inquiry into Road User Charges," Victoria, November 1960.

Published Sources

Barzyk, Fred. *Trucking in a Borderless Market: A Profile of the Canadian Trucking Industry, 1988 to 1994*. Ottawa: Statistics Canada, 1996.

Bess, Irwin. *The Cost of Independence: Socio-economic Profiles of Independent Truck Drivers*. Ottawa: Statistics Canada, 2000.

Chow, Garland. *Labour Standard Issues in the Inter-provincial Canadian Trucking Industry*. Ottawa: Human Resources and Skills Development Canada, 2006.

Craig, Andy. *Trucking: A History of Trucking in British Columbia since 1900*. Saanichton: Hancock House, 1977.

Downs, Art. *Wagon Road North*. Revised edition. Surrey: Heritage House Publishing, 1993. Originally published in 1960.

Drushka, Ken. *Working in the Woods: A History of Logging on the West Coast*. Madeira Park: Harbour Publishing, 1992.

Evans, Rhys. "Looking at the World Through a Windshield: A Historical Geography of the Trucking Industry in British Columbia." MA thesis, Department of Geography, UBC, 1996.

Francis, Daniel. *A Road for Canada: The Illustrated Story of the Trans-Canada Highway*. Vancouver: Stanton, Atkins & Dosil, 2006.

French, Diana. *The Road Runs West: A Century Along the Bella Coola/Chilcotin Road*. Madeira Park: Harbour Publishing, 1994.

Governments of Canada and BC. *Final Report of the Federal-Provincial Task Force on the Transportation and Industrial Relations Issues Related to the Movement of Containers at British Columbia Lower Mainland Ports*, October 26, 2005.

Harvey, R.G. *Carving the Western Path: By River, Rail, and Road Through BC's Southern Mountains*. Surrey: Heritage House, 1998.

———. *The Coast Connection*. Lantzville: Oolichan Books, 1994.

———. *Head On! Collisions of Egos, Ethics, and Politics in BC's Transportation History*. Surrey: Heritage House, 2004

Independent Trucker, "The History of Trucking in British Columbia," September 1988.

Karolevitz, Robert F. *This Was Trucking: A Pictorial History of the First Quarter Century of the Trucking Industry*. New York: Bonanza Books, 1966.

Mayhew, Daniel R. *Commercial Vehicle Driver Licensing Standards in British Columbia*. Ottawa: Traffic Injury Research Foundation, 2007.

McConaghy, Mel. *My Life Through a Broken Windshield*. Prince George: North Star Printing and Publication, 2003.

Nix, Fred P. *Truck Activity in Canada: A Profile*. Ottawa: Transport Canada, 2003.

Ontario Trucking Association. *The Golden Years of Trucking*. Rexdale: Ontario Trucking Associaton, 1977.

———. *Trucking and Triumphs: 80 Years of the Ontario Trucking Association*. Toronto: Ontario Trucking Association, 2006.

Rothenburger, Mel. *Friend O' Mine: The Story of Flyin' Phil Gaglardi.* Victoria: Orca Book Publishers, 1991.

Rubak, Paul M. *Big Wheels Across the Prairies: A History of Trucking in Alberta Prior to 1960*. Calgary: BWATP Publisher, 2003.

Statistics Canada. *Trucking in Canada, 2005*. Ottawa: Government of Canada, 2007.

Taylor, G.W. *The Automobile Saga of British Columbia 1864–1914*. Victoria: Morriss Publishing, 1984.

Trainer, Mary. "Canyon Capers Remembered," *Trucking Canada* (June 1986): pp. W20–W25.

Truck World. "British Columbia Trucking Association: Seventy-Five Years of Strength," vol. 5, issue 6, June 1988.

Watt, K. Jane. *Milk Stories: A History of the Dairy Industry in British Columbia, 1827–2000*. Abbotsford: Dairy Industry Historical Society of BC, 2000.

White, Frank. "Hauling Around Town," in Rolf Knight, *Along the No. 20 Line: Reminiscences of the Vancouver Waterfront*. Vancouver: New Star Books, 1980: 73–83.

White, Frank, and Howard White. "How It Was With Trucks," *Raincoast Chronicles First Five*. Madeira Park: Harbour Publishing, 1976: pp. 126–136.

Wihksne, John. "Trucking the Great White North," *Wheels of Time* (March/April 2006): 22–27.

Wise, Bert. *Tales of a BC Trucker, 1935–38*. British Columbia: self-published, 1987.

Index

Harbour Publishing Co. Ltd.
P.O. Box 219, Madeira Park, BC, V0N 2H0
www.harbourpublishing.com

Edited by Pam Robertson
Text design and maps by Roger Handling, Terra Firma Digital Arts
Index by Stephen Ullstrom
Printed and bound in Canada on paper containing 10% post-consumer recycled fibres

Harbour Publishing acknowledges financial support from the Government of Canada through the Canada Book Fund and the Canada Council for the Arts, and from the Province of British Columbia through the BC Arts Council and the Book Publishing Tax Credit.

Additional image credits

Front dust jacket: Sea-to-Sky Highway at sunset—David Nunuk photo.

Back dust jacket: Merchant's Cartage flatbed hauling a Grunman Goose through Vancouver, 1940s—courtesy of Dietmar Krause.

Front flap (clockwise from top left): Cariboo Highway between Spuzzum and Lytton, 1930s—Royal BC Museum, BC Archives, A-04683; Detail from Andy Craig's 1936 Indiana—David Nunuk photo; Jersey Milk horse meets new electric truck, 1950s—Vancouver Public Library 81378, Artray photo.

Back flap (clockwise from top left): George Brooks's Reo pinned in Fraser Canyon—courtesy of Rod Parkinson; McGavin's bread van in front of Vancouver City Hall, 1946—City of Vancouver Archives, CVA 586-4759, Don Coltman / Steffens Colmer photo; Vancouver Transfer truck and driver, 1935—Vancouver Public Library 10690, Leonard Frank photo; Licence plate—Courtesy of Ron Garay; Exhaust pipe detail—Kevin Oke photo; Logging truck crossing bridge—UBC Library, Rare Books and Special Collections, MacMillan Bloedel Ltd. fonds, BC 1930/37/6.

Frontmatter:
Half-title page: British Columbia Electric Co. coke delivery truck, 1926—Vancouver Public Library, 549.
Title page and table of contents: David Nunuk photos.

Timeline (clockwise from top left):
Page 22—Royal BC Museum, BC Archives, A-03867, Frederick Dally photo; Kelowna Public Archives, 3423; Royal BC Museum, BC Archives, B-07901; City of Vancouver Archives, LGN 1264.2; City of Vancouver Archives, CVA 99-5293, Stuart Thomson photo; Royal BC Museum, BC Archives, D-05504; Royal BC Museum, BC Archives, D-09370.
Page 23—City of Vancouver Archives, Trans N20, W.J. Moore photo; Vancouver Public Library 12335, Leonard Frank photo; Vancouver Public Library 33323, Leonard Frank photo; City of Vancouver Archives, CVA 586-3976, Don Coltman/Steffens Colmer photo; Courtesy of Dale Nelson; City of Vancouver Archives, CVA A18712, Stuart Thomson photo; Royal BC Museum, BC Archives, B-06876; City of Vancouver Archives, CVA 99-270, Stuart Thomson photo.
Page 24—Vancouver Public Library 68055, Leon (Lee) Holt photo; Alberni Valley Museum; courtesy of Hank Rabe; Alberni Valley Museum; courtesy of Dietmar Krause; Vancouver Public Library 81378, Artray photo.
Page 25—Vernon Museum & Archives, No. 2853; six others by David Nunuk.

Library and Archives Canada Cataloguing in Publication

Francis, Daniel   Trucking in British Columbia : an illustrated history / Daniel Francis.

Includes index. ISBN 978-1-55017-561-5

1. Trucking—British Columbia—History. 2. Truck driving--British Columbia--History. 3. Truck drivers—British Columbia—Biography. I. Title.

HE5635.B7F73 2012   388.3'2409711   C2012-904259-5